New York's North Country and the Civil War

NEW YORK'S NORTH COUNTRY AND THE CIVIL WAR

Soldiers, Civilians and Legacies

DAVE SHAMPINE

FOREWORD BY HAROLD SANDERSON

THE History PRESS

Published by The History Press
Charleston, SC 29403
www.historypress.net

First published 2012

Manufactured in the United States

ISBN 978.1.60949.651.7

Library of Congress Cataloging-in-Publication Data

Shampine, Dave.
New York's north country and the Civil War : soldiers, civilians and legacies / Dave Shampine.
p. cm.
ISBN 978-1-60949-651-7
1. New York State)--History--Civil War, 1861-1865. 2. New York (State)--History, Local. 3. New York (State)--History--Civil War, 1861-1865--Biography. 4. New York (State)--History--Civil War, 1861-1865--Social aspects. 5. Soldiers--New York (State)--Biography. 6. Soldiers--New York (State)--History--19th century. 7. Civilians in war--New York (State)--Biography. 8. Civilians in war--New York (State)--History--19th century. 9. United States--History--Civil War, 1861-1865--Biography. 10. United States--History--Civil War, 1861-1865--Social aspects. I. Title.
E523.S53 2012
974.7'03--dc23
2012008737

Contents

Contents

Foreword

The American Civil War is seen as the first of the modern total wars. Its effects on the American people were profound. As you read the various narrations presented, I am sure you will gain new insight regarding America's war with itself. You will be struck by the actual experience of army life of the common soldier. This is not a formal history, but by the various perspectives used, it reflects our national consciousness. Bruce Catton, writing in "Why History," explains, "What we shall someday become will grow inexorably out of what we have created in the past." Mr. Shampine gives us historical insight by which the past becomes a poignant lesson for the present.

Those veterans who lived in the twentieth century were recognized and honored and interviewed by the younger generations. When the last veteran passed, a great door was closed, and that veteran locked the door and took the keys with him. No longer would we have a first-person connection with the era of the American Civil War. Today, our connection to that war is well recorded. Thousands of histories and novels, memoirs and movies and prominent documentaries are available to the public.

Locally, memoirs like those of Delevan S. Miller's *Drum Taps in Dixie* and *A Drums Story* present Miller as a twelve-year-old youth from West Carthage, New York. When discharged in 1865, he was a fifteen-year-old veteran of the Civil War. This offering by Mr. Shampine of Civil War memoirs embraces a cross-section of veterans from Northern New York counties. Each memoir is a poignant personal sketch that includes both pathos and irony, bound up in real personal history. Men such as D.S. Miller wrote about how they felt cheated by the war as each lost part of his youth: "When writing home to my family, I could not tell them where he had last seen their boy."

In his extensive memoir *From Bull Run to Chancellorsville*, Newton M. Curtis gives the reader a short description of himself as being taller than President Lincoln. He was the tallest officer in the Union army, and this physical characteristic often drew concern for his safety. He was seriously wounded by artillery fire at Fort Fisher in 1865.

Other aspects of their lives would appear at irregular intervals, and that was their reaction to events occurring at home. The story regarding "Schule Belle" has been touched on many times in the past. This brass bell was sent home to Theresa, New York, to stand in for a school bell lost when the local school burned down during the war. This story represents the ingenuity of various participants in acquiring the bell and its shipment home and is supported by the continued existence of the bell in an honored place in the old Theresa grade school. The two main men involved with this incident spoke very little of the bell after the war. But history tells us that August Kissell and Noah Brooks are seen as the main actors in the event.

Over the years, a few Northern New York men were honored as recipients of the Medal of Honor during the Civil War. Later in life, these men would describe themselves as simply ordinary men for whom fate allowed their personal bravery to shine brighter than anyone around them. They were not alone in receipt of this honor. Doctor Mary Walker from Oswego County was the only woman given the nation's highest honor.

Soldiers' stories are legion regarding active participation in the Civil War. After their lives had spun out, these men passed from the scenes of life. Then their stories resided in old trunks in family attics. Once in a while, their lives would come to light through the inquisitiveness of children and adults seeking links for family history. Now and then, a piece of history comes to light that causes concern about a family member as it reflects negatively when compared to other members of the family. Civil war records are not always accurate. Some documents reveal charges of desertion, but these must be taken with a grain of salt. Today, we know that many of these charges are simply clerical errors.

Recordkeeping during the Civil War was not an exact science. A soldier who was sent to a hospital for any reason was a lost individual, detached from the regiment but not recorded as a patient at any hospital. After thirty days, his regiment presumed the soldier as having deserted, as he had not returned to duty. If the man returned to the regiment, the record was corrected, but some men never returned and their record of desertion stood for many years. Later, if a veteran lived long enough to apply for a pension (1891), this incorrect information would appear again to block a pension application. Some veterans never received a pension because of the red tape created by government bureaucracy.

Widows of veterans were regularly granted pensions but received a mere pittance as their proper share. Many widows remarried, thus forfeiting whatever pension rights to which they were entitled. It is a fact that the last Civil War veteran in Northern New York died in 1944, but the last widow of a veteran died in 1971. Pension benefits had been paid from 1863 until 1971.

Madison Barracks at Sackets Harbor, New York, was a major influence well before the Civil War. A mainstay of naval and land operations during the War of 1812, the base became the depot for recruits from most of Northern New York. Between 1861 and 1865, Madison Barracks processed about twenty-three regiments of volunteers for the Union army.

Stories were told around the campfires on cold nights, and one likely topic was about a man with the Sixtieth New York Infantry out of Ogdensburg, New York, who possessed a permanent leave of absence signed by Major General George H. Thomas. The man's wife was seriously ill and was expected to die soon. The soldier's leave of absence was issued to provide that "the Bearer could remain away until after the death of his wife." Occasionally, he returned to his unit to visit his friends, but his departure from duty became permanent. His wife recovered and lived a good fifty years. Another story tells of a man from the Adams area who was reported killed at Gettysburg. His funeral service was being held when the man walked into the church and reported himself alive, although wounded.

The Grand Army of the Republic, the veterans' civic and social organization, became active in Northern New York in the 1880s and affected many aspects of the veterans' lives for seventy years. The GAR, which played a key role in the founding of Decoration Day, was responsible for the 1891 pension bill that gave its members a veterans' pension. It was the political machine that was the moving force that elected or defeated three presidential candidates late in the nineteenth century.

Map of Watertown, New York, in the mid- to late nineteenth century. *Courtesy Library of Congress.*

Did the veterans view technological changes in America in a positive light? These men felt trapped in a time warp. They continued to live in a vanished world locked in the past. They could not understand or accept electric lights,

the radio or the airplane, which some thought should be outlawed because the airplane was seen as a justification for total war. These developments seemed beyond their grasp.

The Civil War Veterans database housed at Melvil Dewey Library, Jefferson Community College, Watertown, New York, holds more than 20,000 veterans' records. These represent the six northernmost counties of

New York State. The collection reveals that more than 2,700 Northern New York men failed to survive the war. About one-quarter of them were felled on the battlefield, while more than half died from disease.

The database brings to one location the collected histories that have been scattered about in vague or unknown locations. This has allowed researchers and scholars to mine the records for information about the men who went south to help preserve the Union.

Truth is stranger than fiction. After reading these monographs, you may feel that fiction is dead. Mr. Shampine deals objectively with each presentation, and he does not attempt to explain history. What you read is what you get. It is the reader's choice to accept it as written or to determine for oneself that there is more to the stories than what is presented in the pages that follow. Many people form an all-consuming desire to seek more information, and this is what the author encourages from his reading audience. Your journey into the past is recommended, as it will present the reader a cogent view of an America that has quietly slipped away and followed the Civil War veteran into history.

—Harold I. Sanderson, MA/CASAC (Ret.)

Mr. Sanderson authored in 1992 Whispers From the Past, *a product of his early research about north country men who served in the Civil War. He built on that research to create the Civil War Veterans database mentioned above. He holds a master's degree in nineteenth-century history and public policy from New York State University at Albany, where he was an instructor in Canadian history and for a course about division and reunion. Mr. Sanderson also was an instructor at Jefferson Community College, where he continues his Civil War research.*

A Homegrown Patriot

DePeyster Farmer Rises to Civil War Hero and Statesman

As a group of young men, most of them farmers, met on an April evening 151 years ago in the Methodist church at DePeyster, one stood out above all with his six-foot-seven frame. And it was he, the town's twenty-five-year-old postmaster, who was asked to speak.

Newton Curtis—who years later would be a powerful speaker in the political arena—proclaimed, "Patriotism is of no party." Rebuffing a suggestion that political convictions may discourage men from answering President Lincoln's call to bear arms, he exhorted, "The Union must be preserved." Fifteen men vowed to serve that night, and more added their names at a subsequent gathering. Finally, on May 2, 1861, Curtis, the elected captain, was leading a group of at least sixty-four volunteers from DePeyster and Macomb in a parade of farm wagons to Ogdensburg and, ultimately, to the battlefields of the South.

At the conclusion of the Civil War, the tall gentleman—"with a largeness of body, though not adipose or over fleshy," according to the *Canton Commercial Advertiser*—would return home a wounded and decorated hero who had risen to the rank of general. In his future was the politics of St. Lawrence County, New York State, as well as the nation. The "hero of Fort Fisher," as he was lauded, was to become "one of the political war horses" of his day, the Canton paper reported.

Newton Martin Curtis had aspired to public service from the time he was a young man, and he had experienced defeat, even at an embarrassing level

Newton Curtis, the pride of DePeyster, New York. Taken from his autobiography *From Bull Run to Chancellorsville. Courtesy* Watertown Daily Times.

Jonathan and Mary Riser Curtis, parents of Newton Curtis. *Courtesy DePeyster historian Sharon Murdock.*

in DePeyster, his hometown. He was born on May 21, 1835, the second son of Jonathan and Mary Riser Curtis, on his parents' farm. His father, a soldier in the War of 1812, was the grandson of William Curtis, who had come from England in 1632 to settle in Boston.

Newton Curtis was educated in DePeyster schools and at Gouverneur Wesleyan Seminary. He followed his father's trade in farming, but he also studied law.

He was not quite twenty-two in 1857 when he was commissioned DePeyster's postmaster. Three years later, he sought political office, the first assembly district of St. Lawrence County. Running on the Democratic line, the young man didn't have a chance. His 1,424 votes were dwarfed by Republican Charles Richardson's tally of 3,536. DePeyster gave the hometown gentleman a mere 47 votes. Richardson counted 207.

Some of DePeyster's farmers were in Ogdensburg on an April day when they came upon a rally at Ford and Isabella Streets. *Ogdensburg Journal* editor Henry R. James was standing on a dry goods box, reading the president's call for volunteers. They brought the battle cry home, organizing a meeting the night of April 15, 1861, in the Methodist church.

Captain Benjamin Eastman, an old-line Whig, protectionist and active Republican worker, urged attendees to answer the president's call and was taken aback by an apparent lack of interest. He called on Curtis to address the gathering.

"I said that patriotism was of no party, and regretted that the question of party politics should be raised when there was nothing to be considered but the preservation of the Union," Curtis wrote forty-five years later in a book, *From Bull Run to Chancellorsville.*

After the session broke up, discussions continued in Mason's Tavern, where fifteen men volunteered to go to battle. After a second meeting at the town hall on April 26, Curtis found himself elected captain of a full complement of noncommissioned officers, musicians and sixty-four privates.

On May 2, the company of raw recruits gathered at the DePeyster Town Hall for a 7:00 a.m. march, destination Ogdensburg, about eleven miles away. Before leaving, they were presented $400, collected by the women of their community.

As their parade reached Heuvelton, they were greeted by a cheering crowd waving flags and handkerchiefs, as well as a booming cannon. Upon arrival in Ogdensburg, the men were given the first designation of their organization: gingham caps distributed by the district United States attorney. These would do until uniforms were issued.

Then, to the music of two bands, they marched to the Northern Railroad depot, where they boarded a train. Their next stop was Albany, where the group was to become Company G of the Sixteenth New York Volunteer Infantry.

The young men of the Sixteenth trained in Virginia, where in July they were brought together with the Eighteenth, Thirty-first and Thirty-second New York Regiments to form the Second Brigade of the Fifth Division, Second United States Infantry. Off they marched to Fairfax, where on the morning of July 17, 1861, they got their first taste of combat, a small skirmish at which a sergeant with the Eighteenth fell mortally wounded. Ahead of them would be defeat at Bull Run, which, Curtis wrote, was a show of unskilled leadership on both sides. The soldiers from the North pulled back to reorganize for their next encounter.

They marched onward in 1862 into a number of battles. In an exchange between North and South on May 7 at West Point, Virginia, Curtis was wounded. The scene was described by Major Joel J. Seaver in his dispatch to the *Malone Palladium*, of which he was editor: "Captain Curtis, while urging on his men, was struck by a ball in his left breast, directly over his heart. The ball struck a rib, glanced around and came out of his back. Twice he rallied his men after the shot, and, by his presence of mind and bravery, doubtless saved many a valuable life."

In March 1863, Curtis, having been promoted to lieutenant colonel five months after he was wounded, took advantage of his leave of absence to marry Emeline Clark of Springfield, Illinois. He shared no revelations in his book about that episode of his life. It also is unclear how long he permitted injury and wedding bells to keep him away from the battlefield.

The Sixteenth, meanwhile, fought on. There was Gaines's Mill, Malvern Hill and Crampton's Pass, Maryland. At Crampton's Pass, 270 men went into battle, and 209 came out unscathed; 18 were killed and 43 wounded, according to Curtis's book. Then came Antietam and Fredericksburg, followed in the spring of 1863 by Chancellorsville.

"Never was the Sixteenth put into a hotter fight, and never did it show more valor and fortitude than in the battle of Salem Heights (also called Salem Church, the final assault at Chancellorsville), where it contended against overwhelming numbers," wrote Curtis.

In defeat on May 3 and 4, the Sixteenth suffered 20 more deaths and 87 wounded; 49 were listed as missing. That was the unit's last fray. On May 22, 1863, the Sixteenth was mustered out of service. Its final campaign tally was 130 killed in action or mortally wounded and 84 deaths by various other causes.

As he looked back years later to his war experience, Curtis was philosophical about the fear of death as he went into battle: "The fear of death is at best but momentary, and is only felt when it appears imminent; as soon as the crisis is past it is the first thing forgotten." He continued, "I had no fear of death in battle, for before I was mustered into service, I had a presentiment that I should not be killed in the army, but would have my eyesight injured."

And so it came to pass, on January 15, 1865, as he and comrades of the former Sixteenth served under the banner of the 121st New York Volunteer Infantry.

Fort Fisher, at the mouth of the Cape Fear River, below Wilmington, North Carolina, was "the largest and best equipped fortification constructed by the Confederates," he said in an address in 1899 to the Massachusetts Military Order of the Loyal Legion of the United States in Boston. The fort's heavy defensive barriers extended out some twelve feet and were twelve feet high or more, he noted. He described the attack as "a hand-to-hand contest with swords and bayonets":

> *We gained possession of the seventh traverse at 4:45 p.m.…and shortly after 5:15 p.m.…when the sun was just disappearing…while the volunteers were assembling, I went further into the fort and had ascended a magazine or sand dune for the purpose of looking into the angle of the bastion I intended to attack, when I was struck and disabled by two fragments of a shell, one destroying the left eye and the other carrying away a portion of the bone at the base of the brain.*

Brigadier General Adelbert Ames, Second Division commander, wrote, "Bvt. Brig. General N.M. Curtis, commanding First Brigade, was prominent throughout the day for his bravery, coolness and judgement. His services cannot be over-estimated. He fell a short time before dark seriously wounded in the head by a canister shot."

Curtis was presented the Medal of Honor "for extraordinary heroism" in the battle. "The first man to pass though the stockade, Brigadier General Curtis personally led each assault on the traverses and was four times wounded," his citation read.

Fort Fisher fell that night to Union land and naval forces. Confederate general William H.C. Whiting was mortally wounded in the battle, and Colonel William Lamb, commander of the fort, was seriously wounded. Lamb survived, later to write, "Fort Fisher commanded the last gateway between the Confederate states and the outside world. Its capture, with the resulting loss of the Cape Fear River defenses and of Wilmington, the great importing depot of the south, effectually ended all blockade-running."

In 1899, two old soldiers, General Curtis and Colonel Lamb, came face to face on a stage in Canton's old town hall. There to help institute a chapter of Phi Beta Kappa, "Both spoke, paying one another splendid compliments," the *Canton Commercial Advertiser* reported, describing Lamb as "a polished southern gentleman with well trimmed moustache."

Curtis was not a brigadier general at the time of the Fort Fisher assault, but his "gallant services" there prompted Secretary of War Edwin M. Stanton to elevate him to that rank. Following the surrender at Appomattox, Curtis was appointed chief of staff of the department of Virginia and was later

Undated photo of the four daughters of Newton and Emeline Clark Curtis. Their sitting order was not listed. *Courtesy DePeyster historian Sharon Murdock.*

named commander of southwestern Virginia. He ended his military career on January 15, 1866. About one month later, on February 25, Emeline gave birth to the first of the couple's four daughters, Phoebe.

An appreciative government awarded him a string of political appointments over the next eighteen years, beginning in 1866 as collector of customs for the district of Oswegatchie. One year later, he became a special agent with the Treasury Department. The family continued to grow, with Mary born in February 1868, Florence in 1873 and Elizabeth in 1878.

A career in the political arena for the gifted, one-eyed orator, recognized for his commanding stature and soldierly bearing, began in 1884 when he headed into seven successive terms as state assemblyman. Among his accomplishments in Albany was the bill he sponsored that placed the St. Lawrence Psychiatric Center in Ogdensburg. He was elected to Congress in 1890 and served until 1897. His departure from the legislative branch brought another political appointment: inspector of soldiers' homes.

The postwar home of Newton Curtis at 417 Elizabeth Street, Ogdensburg, New York. *Courtesy* Watertown Daily Times.

The retired general and statesman maintained homes at 417 Elizabeth Street in Ogdensburg and at Irving Place, New York City. While walking there the afternoon of January 8, 1910, he collapsed and died. He was seventy-five.

A statue bearing the general's image, created by Roland Hinton Perry, still stands in Ogdensburg. His daughters and 150 Civil War veterans attended the unveiling ceremony on October 2, 1913, in a downpour.

Florence Curtis, a librarian and educator, lived in Richmond, Indiana. She died in October 1944 at the age of seventy-one.

The oldest of the sisters was the only one to marry. When Phoebe Vilas died at eighty-seven in March 1953 in the Elizabeth Street family home, she left three sons: Curtis M. Vilas of Michigan City, Indiana; George C. Vilas of Miami; and Joseph W. Vilas of Madison, Wisconsin.

Mary, who was eighty-three when she died in October 1951, and Elizabeth, a retired teacher who died eleven months later at age seventy-four, lived most of their lives in the family's Ogdensburg home.

Newton Curtis's brother, Gates, who was twelve years older than Newton, gained some notoriety of his own. He wrote a history of St. Lawrence

County, *Our County and Its People* (published in 1894), and was an inventor, patenting several models of the Curtis plow, which he manufactured in his foundry. He also invented a turbine water wheel and a shingle machine.

Gates Curtis died on January 13, 1905, in Ogdensburg.

Watertown Times *librarian Lisa Carr, DePeyster historian Sharon Murdock, Charles Carter,* Watertown Times *reporter David Winters and the staff of the St. Lawrence County Surrogate Court assisted in gathering information for this story.*

Life on the Rock

One-Armed Veteran Found Vocation as Lighthouse Keeper

After little more than ten months in Mr. Lincoln's army, Willard L. Cook came home to Jefferson County, New York, in 1862, concerned that his future, as he put it, "was not pleasant to contemplate."

The Ellisburg, New York native was lacking his right arm, the limb having been amputated after the Second Battle of Bull Run. He saw himself "the bread winner of the family," with wife and four children ages five to thirteen, disabled from working his carpentry trade and "not knowing enough of business matters to gain a livelihood for himself and family." But he resolved, as he penned several years later in his memoirs, to adopt a motto for life: "As the best you can in the circumstances you are in."

After kicking around from one job to another for about seven years, he finally found his place in life: keeper of the Rock Island Lighthouse near Clayton, New York. The question from kin and acquaintances was predictable: with only one arm, someone asked, "How are you going to get about on the river?" He would show them.

Willard was born on July 30, 1823, one of the ten children of John and Abigail Littlefield Cook. After attending Ellisburg-area schools, he graduated at seventeen from Syracuse Commercial College. Charlotte Fox of Clayton became Mrs. Willard Cook, and between 1849 and 1857, the couple was blessed with two daughters, Abbie and Emma, and two sons, Orren and Byron.

Then came the divide between the North and the South. Writing about himself in the third person, Cook recalled, "In October 1861, being past 38 years old, [he] was in the full strength of manhood, felt as though he ought to do something for the support of the best government that the world ever had. There being nothing else that he could do, he enlisted into Company B of the 94th Infantry volunteers, at Madison Barracks," Sackets Harbor, New York.

The regiment, nine hundred strong, dubbed the "Belle Jefferson Rifles," moved out in March 1862, heading for its first detail at Washington, D.C. Even before leaving New York, the regiment suffered its first casualties. Five cars of the train derailed and plunged into the Hudson River, killing five men and committing supplies to the river.

Eventually assigned to Manassas, Virginia, the unit participated in the Battle of Cedar Mountain on August 9, 1862. Later came the Battle of Groveton on August 29 and then, the next day, the Second Battle of Bull Run.

Corporal Cook's brigade was rushed into the fight, he wrote. During a Confederate charge, he suffered a gunshot wound in the elbow joint of his right arm, shattering it. Seeing his brigade in retreat, he scurried to a deep, dry ditch, entered it to get out of the range of enemy fire and placed a bandage around the arm to stop the bleeding. Subsequently, as he held his right hand with his left, he set out to catch up to the brigade. As evening bore down on him, he reached a cabin, where he found three surgeons attending to the wounded. He waited beyond 10:00 p.m., after the surgeons took a dinner break, to have his arm amputated.

The following morning, the soldier, weak from blood loss, walked about three miles to Centerville, Virginia, and there obtained a carriage ride to Washington, thirty miles away.

On September 13, 1862, he became an honorably discharged one-armed war veteran who was uncertain about his future. Applying his skills and soliciting the help of mechanics, Mr. Cook had a hook attached to the stump of his lost arm that, he wrote, proved to be of good service. He bounced around for the next seven years, tackling a variety of jobs. He was doorkeeper at the state assembly and then a book salesman.

"He worked very hard to sell 30 books and deliver them in one month time, just getting enough out of it to pay his expenses," his memoir reported.

He tried being a town tax collector, a recording clerk in the Jefferson County clerk's office and a census worker in the summer of 1865. That led to a short-term position in the state's census department. His career odyssey brought another government job, clerk of the county election board, but soon he was again a traveling salesman. He peddled pictures and frames, patent rights for farm fence gates, books in Michigan and finally, in the spring of 1868, steel engravings. He stuck with that for two years, earning a modest living. But the job called for travel around the state and into Vermont. He tired of being away from his family so much, and "the expenses of a growing family of children that had to be fed, clothed and educated all together kept the finances of Cook in an embarrassing condition."

There was another mouth to feed now, two-year-old Elton Clarence, and their eldest, Abbie, now twenty, had become quite feeble.

While in the Clayton/Cape Vincent, New York region in December 1869, he met an old friend, Richard Esselsteyn, who was collector of customs. Cook was introduced to another customs official, and he inquired about possible employment. The conversation was not forgotten.

"Very soon after, [Mr. Cook] received a letter from his brother, Horace, saying that he could have the Rock Island Lighthouse, and that he had better come and see about it," Mr. Cook wrote. Willard and Charlotte took a horse and cutter at their Belleville home and set out for Clayton, subsequently learning that his friend Mr. Esselsteyn had been campaigning for him. But it wasn't a simple "you're hired" situation. He was instructed to get up a petition of as many influential people as possible to endorse his merits.

His petition was forwarded to the collector of customs at Sackets Harbor, David O. DeWolf, who could make a recommendation to the chief district customs officer. Mr. Cook had an immediate ally. Mr. DeWolf was quartermaster in the Ninety-fourth Regiment and was his buddy in the outfit. "Mr. DeWolf took up this case with a hearty good will, and assured Cook that he was just as sure of the position of lightkeeper as he was to live till the next April," Mr. Cook recalled.

Late in the winter of 1870, a customs official arrived in Cape Vincent to announce that Mr. Cook was to become Rock Island lightkeeper after the first of April 1870.

As the family prepared for island life, they moved their belongings in March for temporary storage at Port Orleans, later-day Fishers Landing, New York. Finally, on April 1, the items were packed aboard rowboats for the half-mile run to the keeper's house on Rock Island. The St. Lawrence River was still iced over, a good eight to ten inches thick, so the channel had to be cut to make way for the transport craft. His next mission: show people that he'd be able to manage maneuvering a boat. "No trouble about that," he wrote. "He set his inventive genius to work, and soon had a plan evolved, that worked very well in practice, so well that Cook subsequently became an expert oarsman." He simply fixed a staple in the oar used by the disabled right arm, and his hook became a substitute for the lost hand, enabling him to row a boat successfully.

A different issue faced the new man on the job. "The new keeper was entirely ignorant of the duties of the position." No printed instructions were anywhere to be found in the lighthouse, which dated back to 1853, so he and his son Byron set out in an old skiff, heading two miles downriver to visit the last keeper, Joseph Collins. Mr. Collins's wife made the return trip with them and enlightened Mr. Cook about the routine that would be his for about nine years.

From his little perch on the St. Lawrence, Mr. Cook was able to view the early development of Wellesley Island, today's centerpiece for the Thousand Islands Bridge crossing to Canada. When he first saw "Well Island," as he referred to it, the island

> *was nearly all covered with original forest trees. There were only three poor old houses and one of them a log house in sight of the lighthouse, making it a lonely place to be shut up in for the family who had just moved from Belleville, where they enjoyed the privilege of good religious society and good schools. In fall of 1874, Thousand Island Park Association was formed, and they purchased 700 acres of wild land at the head of Well Island and a semi-wild farm of 200 adjoining. In spring 1875, they began building their park. Enabled family to attend many Sunday preaching services by celebrated Divines, also very many intellectual feasts of popular lectures and concerts, all of which made life on the lighthouse island durable in the summer pleasure season.*

Sending their children to school "was a source of anxiety and with expense and extra work," Mr. Cook wrote. During the summer, they were boated to the mainland and brought back after school.

> *It worked well in good weather, but was bad in stormy rough times. The worst feature of the schooling enterprise was in the winter. Towards fall of the first season a plan was suggested by the mother that they move to Clayton for winter schooling. A permit was needed from lighthouse inspector to move off island. He* [Mr. Cook] *wrote request, and the favor was*

> *granted, about a half-month before time for closing. The family was moved, and the light keeper stayed and kept the light til navigations closed.*

Clayton school trustees needed some convincing to go along with the arrangement, however. Concerned about the residency issue, they maintained that the Cook children could not attend Clayton schools. Mr. Cook wrote to the superintendent of instruction in Albany. Quickly, Clayton was obliged to accept the Cook children.

Moving off the island in the fall and returning in the spring "was a good deal of trouble, as it was done when river navigation was at its worst," he wrote. And the expenses in Clayton, he revealed, were "about $50 a year."

In his first eight years on the river, he would later chronicle, Mr. Cook was absent only twenty-five in-season nights. "The first absence was in November 1870 of four nights to attend the last sickness and funeral of his mother," he wrote.

Apparently the lighthouse keeper couldn't take time for the June 20, 1871 birth of another daughter, Nettie, because, in his own words, "the second [absence] and last was in April and May of 1876 which was 21 days and nights taking care of his wife during her last sickness, which terminated in her death on the 7th day of May 1876." He returned to duty three days later. "Keeper's two daughters left the station for their home, each taking with them a child of the keeper to live with them, thus leaving the keeper alone at the station to perform his duties as best he can."

He occasionally reflected on being alone. In one such moment, he penned, "The last month nearly have been spent alone, since the family moved to Clayton. Not a living human soul except the keeper has set foot on the island until today for over three weeks. This is solitude in good ernest."

He wasn't always alone, though, like on July 16, 1872: "Weather hot and dry. Flies still continue to inspect the light nights and do not pay any attention to the placard of instructions to visitors, but will persist in lighting and walking on the glass of the lantern, to the great annoyance of the keeper, who has used all the gentle means he is master of, for their removal. Has even used hand and feather brushes as arguments to persuade them to leave, but all to no purpose."

Or a moment on May 10, 1875: "A wild duck flew through one of the plate glass of the lantern, breaking the center of the glass large enough to let the duck through into the lantern, where the keeper caught him. It injured the duck so badly that the keeper killed him the next morning, and also had to put in a new plate glass."

A memorable day for the keeper was August 2, 1872: "Today President U.S. Grant and wife, General Sheridan and Mr. Pullman passed down the river at 8 o'clock p.m. in a steam yacht, destination to Pullman's island near Alexandria Bay. It is understood that President Grant is out for a pleasure excursion and not to swing around the circle for the purpose of making speech. Such a wonderful man."

Things were not always monotonous. For instance, when Cook first took on the job, there was no steamboat landing for passengers in the vicinity. "A steamer captain had a passenger route from Cape Vincent to Alexandria Bay, and made arrangements with Cook to take passengers off his boat [onto a skiff] and set them ashore. The boat was to blow her whistle in time for Cook to get out there with his boat to take such as wanted to go ashore. The plan worked well with no mishaps."

But there was the occasional challenge, like the day when a very short, three-hundred-pound man needed the assist, along with his invalid wife. Mr. Cook always had a ladder handy, particularly to assist the ladies. "It was a risky piece of work to take them down out of the steamboat into a skiff. The river was smooth. A sailor got down into the skiff and held it steady. Others held the top of the ladder and steadied it while [the couple] descended to the skiff. All done safely."

And there was the day when "a sailor was knocked overboard from a schooner, freighted with lumber, about a mile above the station. The vessel was bound across the river in a fair wind. The captain didn't stop vessel to pick up the man, but threw off some lumber for him to cling to, lowered the yawl boat, and sent two men to rescue him and take him to the lighthouse, considerably exhausted. The three stayed until the man was rested, then went down the river to catch up with the schooner."

Less than six months following Charlotte's death, on September 26, 1876, Mr. Cook remarried, taking the widow Jane Connant Taylor as his wife. "Keeper married today…on board the Steam Yacht Hermie while running below Fredrick Island towards Fishers Landing at 12½ o'clock p.m. Took dinner at Grand Central and returned to lighthouse after dinner to be ready for duty as light keeper."

Mr. Cook's former carpentry trade helped bring in some extra cash. He bought an oar plank and went to work to make a good pair of oars. "From this beginning he took up the work for a pastime," he wrote. "He followed oar making as a source of revenue until his strength failed by reason of advancing age. Not long after he began to make oars, he was rated by river oarsmen as the best oar maker on the river. Made about 100 pairs, sold for up to $4 a pair." He proudly revealed that one pair of his oars accompanied a boat that was sent to Washington, D.C., in 1876 for the nation's centennial celebration.

Mr. Cook retired as keeper of the lighthouse in February 1879. He was fifty-five. Willard and Jane made Fishers Landing their retirement home for the next twenty-two years, until February 24, 1901, when the second Mrs. Cook died.

Willard married again the following year, with Dorcas Caswell Connant becoming his final partner in life. He died on February 14, 1916, and Dorcas passed fifteen months later.

Our appreciation goes to Kevin A. Kieff, director of the regional New York State Office of Parks, Recreation and Historic Preservation, for suggesting Rock Island Lighthouse and assisting with source material, as well as to Mark Wentling, whose website (rockislandlighthouse.org) is a wealth of information. The book Whispers From the Past *by Harold I. Sanderson was consulted for information regarding the Ninety-fourth Regiment.*

A Civil War Father and Son Killed by the Same Shell

The scene may have looked like this: an eighteen-year-old Union soldier sits near the wreckage of the battle at Fredericksburg, Virginia, with tears welling in his eyes, writing the crushing news to his mother back in Jefferson County—both his father and brother are dead.

The writer was Nelson W. Randall. Both John Z. Randall, forty-seven, and Artemus A. Randall, twenty, had been felled by a Confederate-fired shell—the same shell, in fact.

The War Between the States was in its twentieth month when President Abraham Lincoln's army suffered a convincing and discouraging defeat on December 13, 1862, at Fredericksburg. The battle left behind many weeping widows and mothers. Among them was thirty-eight-year-old Almena Randall of Woods Mills in the town of Wilna. With the three men in her family gone to war, two of them now dead, she was managing the family farm and tending to her thirteen- and three-year-old daughters. There is little record to be found of Mrs. Randall, but county census records indicate that she must have stood strong despite her losses.

The migration of New Englanders into the woods of Northern New York in the late eighteenth century brought a Vermont couple to settle in Herkimer County. William Randall and his wife had five children, the second of whom was also named William. The junior William married Amanda Ross, who would bring eleven children into the world.

John Randall (with Artemus Randall, inset). *Courtesy of Judith Maclean, Olympia, Washington.*

One of the eleven was John Zinah Randall, born on May 17, 1815. When John was twenty-five, he married Almena Brooks, who was about sixteen when they exchanged vows on November 17, 1840. Their firstborn son, Artemus Asahel Randall, born on March 3, 1842, was named for one of John's brothers who had died in infancy.

Nelson was born on February 22, 1844, and five years later, on March 11, 1849, the couple's first daughter, Esther, arrived.

This Randall family made Woods Mills their home in March 1852, when John spent $340 for a plot of land along the Indian River that he bought from John G. Hubbard, husband of one of his older sisters, Clarina.

Mr. Randall expanded his property with acquisitions in 1853 and 1855, putting together a 150-acre farm on which he was producing twenty-five bushels of wheat, forty bushels of oats, seven bushels of corn and forty pounds of wool, according to the county's 1860 census. He had three horses, six cows, two pigs and four "other cattle," which were probably sheep for wool.

Almena, meanwhile, added a new member to the family on July 27, 1859, in the person of Ella A. Randall. Ella was just shy of three months old when, hundreds of miles away from this tiny, isolated rural community, an incident occurred that would indirectly shape her future. On October 17, 1859, a band of eighteen abolitionists and their leader, John Brown, overtook an arsenal at Harpers Ferry, Virginia, as a means of encouraging slaves to rebel. Brown was captured the next day and was later hanged for treason.

A nation already at odds over slavery was drawn closer to conflict. The rift widened toward the inevitable in December 1860, when South Carolina seceded from the Union, leading the way to a new Confederate States of America. Confederate troops attacked Fort Sumter in the harbor of Charleston, South Carolina, on April 12, 1861. Three days later, President Lincoln issued a call to loyal states for troops.

Nelson Randall. *Courtesy of Judith Maclean, Olympia, Washington.*

Loyalists in the north country were quick to respond. One unit that began to form the very next month was the Thirty-fifth New York Volunteer Infantry Regiment. Young men signed up with various companies of the new regiment in Watertown, Copenhagen, Adams, Redwood, Brownville and Theresa, where Company C was formed.

On September 27, Nelson Randall, then seventeen, committed himself to the cause in Theresa. Two days later, his older brother, Artemus, followed suit. By then, the regiment had already gone to Washington and was joining the Army of the Potomac.

From August 16 to September 2, 1862, the Jefferson County regiment participated in General John Pope's campaign in Virginia, seeing action in battles at Rappahannock River, Sulphur Springs, Gainesville, Groveton, Bull Run and Fairfax Courthouse.

On September 1, 1862, ten days before the regiment entered the bloody Antietam Campaign, John Z. Randall followed his sons to war. "He was a most brave and noble man, whose patriotism alone induced him to take up arms," the *Carthage Republican* later reported.

Confederate troops retreated in defeat from Antietam on September 17. Sharing in a taste of victory, the Thirty-fifth Regiment set off en route to the command of General Ambrose E. Burnside. Destination: Fredericksburg.

A correspondent for the *New York Reformer*, calling himself "Budlong," set the stage for readers in Watertown:

> *You can imagine our position by supposing that the rebels had 100 cannons planted on the hills south of Watertown, and that our army had crossed Black River, and were obliged to engage those batteries; and as we progressed up the river, new and hidden pieces were brought to bear upon us from the bluffs and from the woods in front.*

On the morning of December 10, General Burnside began a daylong assault with his artillery. By day's end, three pontoon bridges had been placed, and Union soldiers were entering the flaming city of Fredericksburg. Some Confederate resistance the following day failed to tarnish the apparent Union victory.

Then came Saturday morning, December 13, 1862. Budlong wrote:

> *About 6 o'clock, after having sufficient time for eating our breakfast, the troops commenced deploying and by 9 o'clock had taken the position assigned them. So thorough was General Burnside's plan of battle that not only every division but every brigade had been assigned a position. At 8 o'clock the order was given to advance and the long lines of infantry, as far as the eye could reach, moved majestically forward. Instantly the whole hills shook and the earth trembled as the rebel batteries spoke from hill tops, where 50 cannons commanded us to pause.*

Union artillery and cavalry maneuvered to support the infantry.

> *We moved up and down our lines, ready to support the weakest points, in full view and in range of the enemy's guns. The majority of their shells passed over our heads, but occasionally bursting in our ranks, removing one or two files. Men were struck while removing the wounded from the field. Generals and colonels were killed and aids* [sic] *were hurled to the earth, such was the carnage of battle. The majority of the officers pronounced this cannonading as heavy and galling as any they have witnessed.*

The men of the Thirty-fifth showed their courage, Budlong wrote:

> *Scarcely any anxiety was manifested, so intent was every one upon obeying orders and remaining firm in their places. When shells burst in Co. A and C, the men nearest the unfortunate only turned their heads to behold the fate of their companions.*

At about 3:00 p.m., the soldiers of the Thirty-fifth were ordered to lie down to try to avoid the continuing barrage of Confederate shells, Nelson Randall noted in his letter home. The *Carthage Republican*, using Nelson's letter, reported:

> *While lying there, a shell struck John Z. Randall on the left shoulder and tore his body asunder, killing him instantly. The same shell struck his son Artemas* [sic] *and carried away his right leg at the knee and tore the flesh from the left, above the knee.*

Artemus Randall died the next day.

The toll paid by the Union army that weekend was 1,180 dead and 2,145 missing. There were 9,028 wounded. For the victorious Confederates, 579 were dead, 127 missing and 3,870 wounded.

Despite the slaughter, the Thirty-fifth actually got out of the battle relatively intact, according to a history of the unit written in 1887: "Their position there, upon the extreme left of the line, where there was little infantry engagement, saved them from the awful slaughter of the right and center." Six of the unit's members were killed; two more died later, including Artemus, and fifteen were wounded. Nelson Randall apparently was among the wounded. He was mustered out of his unit on January 24, 1863, listed as disabled.

The Thirty-fifth was subjected to no more combat. The unit took up winter quarters on the Potomac and then was assigned to provost duty along the Aquia Creek and Fredericksburg Railroad until May 1863, when its service ended.

The Randall father and son were given temporary battlefield burials. Their remains were later returned home for permanent interment, but exactly where they were buried is puzzling. There are monuments standing for them in both Sandy Hollow Cemetery in Philadelphia and in Woods Mills Cemetery, which is now a part of Fort Drum. "They fought for their country, noble and brave, on the battlefield of Fredericksburg, they fought to save," their Sandy Hollow monument reads.

The farm that Almena Randall continued to operate despite the loss of her husband and son apparently grew, although modestly. The 1865 county census shows that three acres had been added to the property, and the number of cows being milked had more than doubled to thirteen by 1864, yielding 2,572 gallons of milk.

Almena had two horses, three swine and four chickens. Her land was giving her twenty-five tons of hay, 15 bushels of corn, 75 bushels of oats and 115 bushels of potatoes. She made 450 pounds of maple sugar from the sap of her maple trees.

Almena Randall. *Courtesy of Judith Maclean, Olympia, Washington.*

On Christmas Eve 1868, Almena began a new life, marrying William K. Peck. In doing so, she likely forfeited her war widow's pension, which even in her day may not have been much of a sacrifice. Such pensions have been found to range from two to eighteen dollars annually. Since her husband had been a private, she was on the lower end of the benefit scale. However, she kept her property and added to it in 1870, purchasing the holdings of her surviving son and his wife of three years, the former Ellen P. Smith.

Almena Randall Peck outlived her second son as well. Nelson moved to Nyack, where for eight years he operated a molding mill. He then relocated to Hoboken, New Jersey, where he purchased a planing mill. On December 22, 1892, at the age of forty-eight, he was killed by machinery in his factory.

Mrs. Peck died on June 1, 1896. Her youngest child, Ella, who was married in 1885 to Silas Monroe, moved to Seattle, Washington, where she died on November 21, 1923.

The last survivor from the John and Almena Randall family was Esther, who on October 25, 1870, became the wife of William H. Ormiston. The couple had a son, who may have been named for Esther's brother Artemus, and a daughter, Ruth, who became the wife of Wilson J. Hastings.

The only descendants of John and Almena Randall still living in the north country, to my determination, are from the line of Ruth Ormiston Hastings. Of her four children (she also named a son Artemus), her son Ernest became the father of Dewey K. Hastings, a resident of Ogdensburg. Mr. Hastings's daughter, Wanda Livingston, the great-great-great-granddaughter of the Civil War couple, also lives in Ogdensburg.

Gathering information about a nineteenth-century farmer is no easy task, especially when he was not active politically. I gratefully acknowledge the valued assistance of Harold I. Sanderson, author of Whispers From the Past: A Source Book of Civil War Veterans from Jefferson County*; Town of Wilna historian Laura M. Prievo; Benjamin J. Cobb, county records management coordinator; Judith Maclean, a great-great-granddaughter of John and Almena who lives in Olympia, Washington; and Esther I. Daniels,* Times *librarian.*

Files in the Jefferson County Surrogate Court and material compiled by Rensselaer A. Oakes in his 1905 Genealogical and Family History, County of Jefferson *also proved most useful. Mr. Oakes, a Watertown newspaperman and magazine writer, died at age sixty-nine in April 1904, several months before his history was published.*

A variety of source material interchangeably spelled the dead Civil War son's name as "Artemus" and "Artemas." The family's recent genealogy, compiled by Judith Maclean, has him as "Artemas," but Mr. Oakes spelled it "Artemus."

During her search through microfilm for newspaper reports about the Battle of Fredericksburg, Mrs. Daniels came across an item that appeared on Christmas Day 1862 in the Jefferson County Union*: "The following report of the killed, wounded and missing in the 94th Regiment has been forwarded to us by Lieut. Charles E. Hulbert, Acting Adjutant: Killed—Co. A, A.A. Larkins, shot in the breast; David Shampine, shot in the head."*

The latter war victim was nineteen. Any relation to the author is unknown.

Handshake with History

Mannsville Woman Witnessed Battle of Gettysburg, Greeted Lincoln

Ninety-year-old Emma Warren Woodard sat with a reporter on her front porch, shading herself from the sun and heat on a June day in 1938, telling the story she had recounted so many times before. A much sought-after speaker in her adopted community of Mannsville, Emma said that she was not at all interested in a proposed trek to her childhood home in Pennsylvania—the site of her claim to fame—to make yet another guest appearance.

"I'd rather not be there," she told *Watertown Daily Times* writer Nathan M. Wood, who was a third her age. "I would have to be up on a platform with a lot of distinguished people and they would be sure to ask me to say a few words, and I just couldn't do it in front of all the crowd that will be there." The upcoming occasion was the seventy-fifth anniversary of the Civil War's bloody Battle of Gettysburg. Emma had lived on the edge of the battlefield, had heard the whiz of passing bullets and cannonballs and had helped tend the wounded. What was most memorable to her, though, was shaking hands with President Abraham Lincoln after he made his celebrated Gettysburg Address.

Mr. Wood, who was in his fourth year as a *Times* reporter, found Mrs. Woodard still able to do her own housekeeping in the South Main Street home where she lived alone. The previous summer, he reported, she had still managed to tend a garden. Several years earlier, she had cataract surgery, but it hadn't kept her from being an ardent reader, keeping up on current affairs. She had given a number of newspaper interviews, but Mr. Wood was likely her last. In another nine months, she would pass into history. The story that follows is taken not only from the Wood account but also from a blend of previous interviews, one undated and three with the *Times* in 1926, 1929 and 1934.

During "the war of the '60s," Emma said, "life in Gettysburg…went on much the same as in peacetime, although rumors of the enemy approaching were as plentiful as rumors today." She reminded her interviewer, "In those days we had no such things as telephones and radio. Our news had to come to us by word of mouth. We had heard so many false rumors of impending attacks that it became like the old story of wolf, wolf. After a time we just paid no attention."

The citizens kept most of their household effects packed and ready to move in case invaders arrived. After all, the Mason-Dixon line was just seven miles to the south. And as the day approached for a collision of armed foes here, Gettysburg was "raided" by both armies.

The residents were all required to furnish supplies for the opposing armies. One of the generals required, among other things, twelve barrels of sauerkraut, recalled Emma, who had been fifteen years old at the time.

As in any Union enclave along the Rebel rim, community members were discouraged by the Union army's failures at Bull Run and Chancellorsville. So, mass meetings were the order of the day, with noted speakers brought in to instill hope and confidence.

But on the night of June 30, 1863, on the eve of the great fight that was to follow, any words of encouragement were drowned out by sounds off in the distance, the sounds of Confederate soldiers "in high spirits, and singing and shouting prevailing," she said.

In the morning, at about 9:00 a.m., booms of cannons began echoing in the air. Emma's mother, Elizabeth Huff Warren, was talking to a soldier—the color of his uniform is unspecified—outside the family's home on West Railroad Street, at the north edge of Gettysburg where the Hanover branch railroad line ended.

"I fear they are going to have a battle right here," Mrs. Warren said.

"No," the soldier tried to assure her, "they are only trying their guns."

"About this time, my father appeared on the scene and said, 'Mother, what are you doing out here with these children? Don't you know there is a battle on?'"

Mrs. Warren told him what the soldier had said. David Warren knew better. He barricaded the house with boards and logs and then dispatched

An illustration of President Lincoln at Gettysburg. *Courtesy* Watertown Daily Times.

his wife and seven children into the cellar. He was right to have done so. Their home was soon in the midst of the first day's fighting, on July 1, 1863. While cowering in the basement with her three brothers and three sisters, Emma heard cannonballs strike in their yard.

"The shells had an unearthly sound," Emma reported. "They screeched as they came toward one and then made a sharp 'zup' as they struck. Father was standing in the doorway when a shell landed close. He threw himself backward to the floor, landing on top of my young brother. My mother came running into the room and when she saw father and baby stretched out on the floor she thought they had been hit. It was laughable afterward."

At the height of battle, a Union soldier tried to hide in the Warren home, saying that his boots rubbed his feet so much that he couldn't possibly run any farther. The last Emma saw of him, she related with a smile, was when he disappeared over a hedge carrying his boots, with the Rebels hot on his heels.

Among the Union fighters in this first day's exchange in Emma's neighborhood were men of the 147th New York Volunteer Infantry from Oswego. They had organized on August 25, 1862, in Oswego. A week later, Orson J. Woodard, who would be assigned the rank of lieutenant, became an enlistee of the unit's E Company at Ellisburg. Earlier in the summer of 1863, the volunteers had become a component of the Second Brigade of the First Corps, and now they were suffering heavy losses as they fell back to Cemetery Hill. Lieutenant Woodard escaped injury.

When the barrage of artillery fire ended late in the day, the family emerged from their shelter. They saw that the Union men had been driven back, and the "Johnnies" had taken control of the northern part of town. "Soon the wounded began pouring into the town, some on stretchers, some on foot, some strapped to horses; some swearing, some praying, all pleading for water," Emma said. All of them, she added, were "black with the grime of battle." Elizabeth Warren and her children mercifully gave water to the wounded.

Opposite the Warren home was a general store. On another corner was the Western Maryland Railroad depot, and another building stood nearby. All of these were made into temporary hospitals as the wounded men flocked in: "Some of my brothers and sisters and I went over and fanned the wounded men, and tried to keep the flies off them. It was a hot day, and the flies swarmed all over the place. We children carried water to the men. We had one cow and in the evening we took milk to the wounded."

That evening, a Rebel soldier, probably no older than sixteen, sat down on the ground in their yard and began to cry. Emma approached him and asked if he was homesick.

"Yes, you have chickens in the yard and we had chickens at home, too," he said.

She asked why he had "wanted" to come to do battle.

"I didn't want to," he said. "I had to."

An officer rode his horse into the yard, asking for something to eat. David Warren, obviously a Union sympathizer, said to his wife, "There is not a bite of anything in the house to eat, is there?"

She answered, "There was a crust of bread in that cupboard. I don't know as it is there now."

"I am so hungry," said the soldier, "I would be glad to eat a piece of dead dog."

Mr. Warren and the officer subsequently sat and talked late into the night, discussing their respective philosophies regarding the issues that had brought them together. As the two men talked, Mrs. Warren began to cry in her home. "They'll take your father," she complained to Emma. "You know he will say just what he thinks and they will take him."

Finally, the officer settled down on his blanket to get some much-needed sleep, and Mr. Warren returned to find his wife sobbing. "He's as fine a man as I ever talked with," Mr. Warren assured her. "He has his ideas and I don't blame him, and I have mine and he doesn't blame me."

The Warrens had an old horse, Fanny, in their barn, and early the next morning, Mr. Warren saw it being led away by a Confederate.

"And behold, there stood the same officer who had eaten the last crust," Emma said. "Father said to him, 'This is rather bad, to give a man your last crust and then see his men take away your only horse.'"

"Is this the only horse you have?" the officer asked. He then called to the soldier leading the horse to halt. "Give this man that horse," he ordered.

"Was this not bread cast upon the waters?" Emma asked. "We kept that horse until the war was over."

The battle roared on for two more days, with the tide turning to the favor of the men in blue. The Warren family, meanwhile, no longer needed to

Emma Warren Woodard shook the president's hand. *Courtesy* Watertown Daily Times.

retreat to their cellar. Combat had moved away from their neighborhood. On day three, the hungry Confederate army led by Major General George E. Pickett with his Virginia troops risked a desperate plunge up Cemetery Hill and lost.

"After Pickett's charge, a thousand dead men and half as many horses lay on the field of battle. It was hot and they had to put them under the ground" in trenches, Emma said.

The public school became a hospital, the lower floor for Southern soldiers and the upstairs for the Union's wounded, she said. As fast as they died, she said, they were buried in the schoolyard: "When colder weather came in the fall, the bodies were taken out and placed in white pine boxes, before they were again buried in 22 sections of the national cemetery. My father was one of the men who had charge of that work." She attended several of the burials.

Four months later, on November 19, 1863, President Lincoln was in Gettysburg to dedicate "the great battlefield." The main speaker of the day, Edward Everett, spoke for more than two hours. Following the dedication, according to a *Times* story in 1934, Emma "saw Mr. Everett go up to President Lincoln following the exercises and heard him say, 'Mr. Lincoln, I would gladly trade my 40-page speech for your 20 lines.'"

After having dinner that evening in the home of his host, Judge David Wills, President Lincoln greeted people during an informal reception. Well-wishers were invited to form in line and shake hands with the president. "The whole family went to the reception," Emma said. "President Lincoln stood on the steps at the York Street door and greeted everyone who came. Father made my little brother, John, shake hands with the president. John was only 3 years old then, and he cannot remember the event." She said that she dropped in line and soon was shaking the hand of the president.

Many of the people who were welcomed into the greeting line that evening were African Americans, she said. Before a divided nation turned Gettysburg into a battlefield, Emma was a fourteen-year-old teacher in a Sunday school in one of the community's two African American churches. The black girls in her class affectionately called her Miss Emma. She continued to teach, spending twenty-two years at the Gettysburg high school. Finally, at forty-five, she met the man of her future in July 1893. The former lieutenant, Mr. Orson Woodard, was in town for a reunion of his 147th Regiment on the thirtieth anniversary of the great battle.

Lincoln's Gettysburg Address. *Courtesy Library of Congress.*

They married the following year, on June 19, 1894, at seven o'clock in the morning. Afterward, Emma bid goodbye to family and friends and was off to her new life in Mannsville. Their home was on South Main Street. Mr. Woodard was a prominent businessman, operating a gristmill where feed, cider and even coal and lumber could be purchased. He lived to the day of their twenty-seventh anniversary, according to several *Times* stories, dying on June 19, 1921. The couple had no children.

Emma Woodard owned property on Chambersburg Street in Gettysburg, and she retreated there shortly after her husband's death, selling the homestead in Mannsville. Her departure lasted about a year. She came back to Mannsville and bought another house on South Main Street, where she would reside until her death.

The Miss Emma of Gettysburg took on a new name with children in Mannsville. Always a participant in patriotic programs of the school and churches, she became known as "Auntie Woodard." Newspapers chronicled the activities of this living monument to the past century. In February 1928, when she had a prominent role in the Parent Teacher Association, she preferred being drawn to school on a sled by some of the children instead of enjoying an automobile ride.

Nine months later, on Armistice Day, she was a guest at Emmanuel Congregational Church in Watertown to give a reading of the Gettysburg Address, even if she might not have heard the original version. Emma also made a trip to Gettysburg shortly after her January 12 birthday in 1929. "This year she will spend Lincoln's birthday in the place where she shook hands with him," the *Times* reported. "She has friends and relatives in Gettysburg and many of the merchants of that place are boys who went to the school where she taught…She has stated that she can remember how Lincoln looked on that occasion where he stood and how impressed she was at shaking hands with the great president of the United States." She was gone for two months. During her trek into nostalgia, she visited the Presbyterian church where Lincoln attended a service and sat in the same pew that Lincoln had occupied with Judge Wills. In an observance of Lincoln's birthday in 1932, she addressed the Mannsville grange about the day she shook hands with the president. That was again her topic at a public reception celebrating her birthday in January 1933.

In her final year, Emma's eyesight gradually abandoned her. She became ill on Wednesday, March 8, 1939, and three days later, at 10:30 a.m., she died in her home. She was ninety-one.

I was at a loss in an attempt to learn more about Orson Woodard. The *Times* usually presented detailed obituaries for Civil War veterans, but a search on microfilm of dates surrounding his reported date of death revealed no story about Mr. Woodard. His monument at Maplewood Cemetery, Mannsville, does not display his date of death, and the real puzzler is that there is no estate file for him in Jefferson County Surrogate Court. A businessman and property owner should have had a probate file.

Photographs of Emma Woodard are a rare find. "About one thing she is very determined and the pleas of her friends are unable to change her mind, Mrs. Woodard will not have her picture taken," the *Times* reported in 1938.

At least 140 men from Northern New York died at Gettysburg or later from their wounds, according to Harold Sanderson, Alexandria Bay, whose Civil War compilations include a website and his book *Whispers From the Past.*

This writer took special note upon discovering Nathan Wood's byline on an Emma Woodard story. I received a letter from Mr. Wood in 1986 while researching the history of the *Watertown Daily Times*. "It was there that I got my start, at the bottom of the Depression, in what turned out to be an exciting, challenging and rewarding career in journalism," he wrote. "The starting pay for a reporter in Depression 1934 was an even $20 a week."

Mr. Wood left the *Times* in 1941 to join his brother-in-law, Floyd J. Rich, at the *Carthage Republican Tribune*. His career took him to Michigan and then San Diego. He retired in Florida and died in March 1991.

Times *librarian Esther Daniels discovered and researched the Emma Woodard story. I thank Marjorie Joyner of Mannsville and Harold Sanderson for their assistance in this project.*

Northern New York's Underground Railroad

Runaway Slaves Made Stops Here En Route to Canada

Two agents from the Deep South were certain that they were about to snare their runaways. A horse-drawn carriage with its three dark-skinned riders had hustled away from Solomon Currie's house in Russell. Only the moonlight could guide the riders and their shadows in the waning minutes of this Halloween night in 1856.

As the buggy crossed a bridge, it was interrupted by the two strangers brashly shouting orders in their Southern drawl. Turn back to the farmhouse, they commanded. The order was obeyed, but the trio in the wagon made no effort to answer questions shouted by the would-be captors, infuriating the slave chasers. One of the agents grabbed hold of the big man on the buggy, only to determine that this was no runaway slave. It was "Uncle Sol" Currie, his white skin blackened by burnt cork.

Sol's companions were similarly disguised, having successfully pulled off the ruse. In the meantime, runners Zeb Harmer and Zeb's son and niece had slipped away with some Halloween revelers from "Station 201" of the Underground Railroad en route to their next hiding place and onward to the promised land, Canada, where they would be free from prosecution and a return to slavery.

Read about the escape channels for slaves in the years leading up to this nation's Civil War, and you will find that three names stand out: Harriet Tubman, Reverend John Rankin and John Brown.

Harriet Tubman, who in 1849 escaped from a Maryland plantation, became known as "the Moses of her people" because of her courageously

Harriet Tubman in 1911, probably at her home in Auburn. *Courtesy Library of Congress.*

repeated trips to rescue some three hundred slaves. She helped them along the uncharted network of houses, businesses and other hiding places throughout the North to the freedom that awaited in Canada. Miss Tubman settled in Auburn, living until 1913.

Reverend Rankin established the gateway for the network. His home in Ripley, Ohio, was the starting point for some ten thousand fugitive slaves and led to a number of wide-ranging northbound paths, some entering New York State. He was a friend of Harriet Beecher Stowe and an inspiration for her crusading novel, *Uncle Tom's Cabin.*

John Brown is, of course, the martyr of Harpers Ferry, Virginia, although he was also called insane, rash but noble and a "villain of the worst sort." His obsession was abolishing slavery in the nation that espoused "liberty and justice for all." He made his last home in North Elba, at Lake Placid, and willed that to be his final resting place.

Syracuse and Oswego were the hubs of New York's freedom trail, and some abolitionists there are remembered. Because no written records were kept, little is known about champions of the cause farther to the north. After all, helping a runaway slave could be costly. The first Fugitive Slave Act passed by Congress in 1793 specified a $500 fine for rescuing, harboring or hindering the arrest of fugitive slaves, and the law of 1850 increased fines to $1,000 and promised jail time of up to six months.

And who could an abolitionist trust, even so far north of the Mason-Dixon line? His enemies were occasional Southern sympathizers, federal officers who stood to receive large rewards for every fleeing slave they returned and some local officers, sheriffs and deputies with high-minded ideas of law enforcement. It would be in his own best interests, then, for the "stationmaster" to keep his secret even from family. Such a story was told about the first "station" across the Jefferson County line in St. Lawrence County.

John Johnson, who settled in about 1830 on the Gouverneur-Somerville Road, was by day a wool carder in Gouverneur and Hailesboro mills and by night a transporter of runaway slaves. Reports in the *Watertown Daily Times* noted that he took his "passengers" through Rossie to Hammond for a rendezvous along the St. Lawrence River.

But this activity was unknown to his son, John Brayton Johnson, who had not reached his tenth birthday. As the story goes, carried down through generations of the Johnson family, the youngster awoke a bit thirsty one winter night and decided to silently head downstairs to fetch some water. As he entered a lower room, he found in slumber three black men in front of the fireplace. Retreating to the second floor, the astonished boy awoke his mother, Sally, who then revealed the cause for the visitors' presence.

Word of the Johnsons' efforts eventually spread. A *Times* story written in 1968 reported that Mr. Johnson became the target of sneers from his neighbors. A Southern sympathizer directed a racial insult at him, prompting the elder Johnson to reply, "I have no doubt of your honesty, but you are allowing your loyalty to the constitution to override your humanity. The constitution is of man; humanity of God." The stationmaster John Johnson was the great-great-grandfather of John B. Johnson, eventual editor and publisher of the *Watertown Daily Times*.

There were four main lines of the Underground Railroad in New York, along with "scores of laterals," according to an extensive study reported in January 1940 by the *Oswego Palladium Times*. One of the runs linked to

Philadelphia and Harrisburg, Pennsylvania, while another passed through New Jersey to New York City, continuing up the Hudson and Mohawk Rivers to Utica, Syracuse and Oswego. The third trail connected Gettysburg with Elmira, the Finger Lakes, Morganville and Lockport. A fourth passed from Summit, Pennsylvania, to Buffalo and Niagara Falls by way of Fredonia. An alternate trek from the Philadelphia route went through Wilkes-Barre, Waverly and Montrose in Pennsylvania and then onward to Plymouth, Lebanon, Peterboro, Mexico and Port Ontario in New York. The Oswego account quoted George C. Bragdon of Rochester, who in August 1896 wrote about the runaways harbored by his father near Port Ontario: "I believe they usually went to Cape Vincent, near the mouth of the St. Lawrence, and were taken over to Canada from there."

The first rest stops out of Oswego County were likely in a fifteen-room Georgian colonial home in Aspinwall's Corners, which is south of Henderson Harbor, and in Constableville in Lewis County.

Fugitive slaves "branched north and followed the lake shore up to our corner," said Mary Aspinwall Taggart in a 1932 interview. "Many were the nights that my father, David Aspinwall, would take under cover until the next night Negroes seeking their way along the Underground Railroad system."

Several locations in Lewis County are said to have provided shelter, but most prominent among them was the Jonathan Collins colonial home built in 1803 in Constableville. The builder was a Revolutionary War veteran from Connecticut, and his son, also named Jonathan, was a state assemblyman. In the attic of this structure, a thirty-two- by nine-foot room was concealed by thick wall planks to hide its short-term visitors. Next stop: Watertown. A house that stood on Arsenal Street is the only known harbor for fugitives here. It was built with hollow sides surrounding an attic cistern to permit concealment in what appeared to be a huge vat for storing water, according to a *Times* clipping. Hollow walls on the second floor formed another hiding place, and from the dining room, a secret opening gave access to a cleverly concealed space behind a fireplace.

John Brown was often a visitor to Watertown during the early 1850s, reported a story in June 1900. He came to confer "with such leading abolitionists as the late Elon Holcomb, who died within the last year at the age of 90 years."

The closest we can come to identifying that abolitionist is Elam Holcomb, who died on November 6, 1898, at age ninety-four, at the home of his son,

Elam L. Holcomb, on Lynde Street. He was born in Herkimer County and was a pioneer settler of Watertown, where he was a machinist.

During one of his Watertown visits, John Brown addressed an antislavery meeting on the "village green," now Public Square, with his rostrum being the seat of a big road wagon, reported the 1900 story. He told the gathering that if he had no other weapon with which to defend a fugitive slave, he would knock down the chasers with the Bible and then plead that he had "given the Scripture to the heathen." On his last visit here, Brown registered at the old American House hotel as Shubal Morgan, a name he had previously used in excursions in Kansas.

Near Watertown, in Dexter, the home of Jesse Babcock offered a haven. He came to the area formerly called Fish Island, where he started as cotton mill superintendent, and built his home in 1833. Mr. Babcock later operated a linseed oil mill, converted it to a plaster mill and later erected a flour mill. During the Civil War, he contracted with the Union army to feed recruits at Sackets Harbor. He died in 1874.

The slaves who had a boat ride in their future likely found their next rest on Grenadier Island. A historian for the town of Cape Vincent, Nellie Casler, wrote in 1906 that there was a house with a hidden room on the island that was maintained by Mr. White. The house and its hiding place are said to have come into use again decades later, for the bootleggers of prohibition days. When the runaways departed from the island, Kingston, Ontario, was their destination for freedom.

Another lakeshore escape, cited in 1932 by *Times* history writer Ernest G. Cook, was on the east side of Three Mile Point. "The late John Carlisle spoke of this station when he told about life out on Point Peninsula and thought there was another one located on Point Peninsula, almost on that narrow neck of land that caused Point Peninsula to be a peninsula instead of an island," Mr. Cook wrote. "It is not known just how this station…operated, yet there are quite well-founded stories that have come down through the years about the place."

Those who stuck to land possibly found their way to Oxbow, or so the construction of a large home there indicates. The Benton-Bonaparte house already had its place in history because it was built in 1819 by Dr. Abner Benton, eventual father-in-law of Caroline Bonaparte, illegitimate daughter of Joseph Bonaparte, Napoleon's brother. There were "cells" in the basement believed to have hidden the travelers, but even more interesting is a brick tunnel leading from the basement to the Oswegatchie River. And yes, it could be argued that this also came in handy during prohibition.

After the Johnson house near Somerville, the invisible tracks split, taking some travelers north to South Hammond and others northeast to Gouverneur. South Hammond offered the Webster house, in whose attic a book containing entries about the railroad was reportedly found many years ago.

On the Gouverneur run, there was the home of prominent abolitionist Myron Cushman on Rock Island Road. Then came Richville, where a house built in 1831 by farmer and cheese maker Chauncey Doane provided hiding in a small room in the juncture above three fireplaces.

There was the sidestep to the Currie house at South Russell, a cut through Canton and, finally, a long-awaited stop at Waddington, which probably was also the collecting place for those who hiked past Morristown after leaving South Hammond.

Near Waddington, they found "Temperance Tavern," or the Ralph Chamberlain house. A *Times* story in 1979 quoted local legend that slaves hid behind furniture stored in closets under the eaves of a third-floor ballroom. More protection was offered in archways and cellars of the house erected by Waddington founder David Ogden. The final stateside stop was "Station 206" in the town of Constable, leading to land border crossings in the Fort Covington region.

The story of New York's Underground Railroad is not complete without special mention of John Brown's last home, North Elba. Gerritt Smith, a wealthy abolitionist living in Peterboro, owned land in the Adirondacks and decided to help runaways make a settlement there. He offered in 1846 his North Elba tract piecemeal, according to a *Times* story in 1940. The settlers formed a colony beside a brook, erecting fifteen or twenty flat-roofed log cabins, each having only one window. Under the floor they scooped out a shallow cellar, where they stored potatoes, the principal item of their diet. They erected a tattered red flag embroidered with the name Timbuctoo.

But the settlers could not adjust to the climate, and there were no supplies for them. John Brown was at their side helping them for two years, but then he departed for the campaign that culminated in his October 16, 1859 raid at Harpers Ferry and his subsequent hanging at Charlestown, Virginia.

The colonists eventually drifted away, and shortly after 1850, Timbuctoo was in decay. One family who endured was that of Lyman Epps, who knew Mr. Brown. He presided at annual memorials to Mr. Brown, giving that

John Brown's grave in North Elba. *Courtesy Library of Congress.*

mission up only a few years before his death in November 1942, when he was said to be 102 years old.

The abolitionist John Rankin had a north country link, too. His son, inventor Thomas L. Rankin, settled in Sackets Harbor. Thomas died in November 1915.

My thanks to Jeanne Thompson of Cape Vincent and Times *librarian Esther Daniels for assistance with information contained in this section.*

A Proud Heritage

Watertown's AME Zion Church Traces Roots to Slave Days

Not long before the crackle of gunfire bloodied the rift between North and South, a slave named Henry Robert Barr strayed from a plantation in Kentucky. A trek along the Underground Railroad brought him to freedom in Montreal, but he eventually backtracked to make his home in Watertown, New York.

After the battle lines were drawn, Joseph H. Rickman (like Henry Barr also in his thirties) slipped away from another plantation, possibly in Virginia. He fell into the hands of Mr. Lincoln's army and donned the blue Union uniform, a huge risk for a runaway slave. Although he didn't make his way north via the Underground Railroad, Joseph Rickman also ended up in Watertown.

And there was also Robert Freeman. He was just a boy of ten when he walked away from his master's property, also likely in Virginia, and was befriended by a Union army major. Again, fate would bring him to Watertown.

With these three, and probably a few others, the Thomas Memorial African Methodist Episcopal (AME) Zion Church, at 715 Morrison Street, can proudly trace its heritage—its roots—to runaway slaves. Reverend Roosevelt Baums believes that his church is an outgrowth of an Underground Railroad station established on a former Watertown street, River Street. While promoting his theory, Pastor Baums succeeded in 2001 in having his church added to the National Register of Historic Places.

The Civil War was just a sad memory in 1878 when Reverend Hamilton R. Phoenix began meeting in the homes of his faithful on River Street, associating with the AME Zion "Connection" that had organized in 1796 in New York City. A goal of the "connected church was to support the movement of slaves," Reverend Baums said.

Although the fugitives from the South no longer had to fear bounty hunters of the slave days by the time the Watertown church was founded, "a lot of people didn't read and write," noted Baums. "They didn't know what was going on. They felt they couldn't breathe safely until they reached Canada."

In 1880, the followers of Reverend Phoenix erected a meetinghouse at 446 River Street, which was at a corner joining Court Street. One of his church trustees, who is said to have provided shelter for the pastor, was Henry Barr.

Mr. and Mrs. Barr were joined by two other couples, the Rickmans and the Freemans, in forming a choir. To collect donations for the construction of their new house of worship, they went to various churches in Watertown, singing for the congregations, according to a souvenir program printed by the church in 1943.

It was reported when he died in February 1902 that Mr. Barr arrived in Watertown in 1865. The route he took on the Underground Railroad was unspecified, leaving to conjecture the question of what motivated his move from Montreal to Jefferson County.

He found Watertown suitable to his needs, making a career as a barber while dabbling in laundering and poultry farming. The "professor," as he became known, acquired sufficient wealth to build a large structure housing his home, shop and rooming house. Quite appropriately, the Court Street edifice was dubbed the Barr Block. It is no longer standing.

Joseph Rickman was another trustee of the new church. Separated from his mother on a slave auction block, Mr. Rickman prepared for his escape by stocking a hiding place with food, clothing and shoes, according to an account in the *Watertown Daily Times* after he died on November 1, 1904. When he fled, he traveled only at night, changing shoes early in his hike to throw bloodhounds off the trail. One night, a sentry heard rustling in leaves and prepared to fire his gun. Mr. Rickman was unsure if he was near a Confederate or Union encampment but risked surrender over being shot. To his fortune, he had found a troop of the Fourth Pennsylvania Cavalry. He joined the unit to be a body servant and saw action at Antietam, Cedar Mountain, Second Bull Run, Gettysburg and White Sulphur Springs. "It required some courage for a [runaway slave] to enter the army then," the *Times* reported, because the Confederates would kill "all who were found under arms."

After the war, he worked at a hotel in Washington and then moved to Elmira, where he became acquainted with a printer from Watertown. His new friend brought Mr. Rickman to Watertown, where he eventually owned "a comfortable little cottage" on Elizabeth Street, now Flower Avenue East. Mr. Rickman made a living as a gardener and lawn keeper for homeowners, and he handled other house chores during the winter.

A soldier from the town of Clayton introduced young Robert Freeman to the north country. Mr. Freeman was a frightened boy dodging gunfire in a battle at Jerusalem Crossing in Virginia, "scurrying to and fro…hiding behind trees," according to his August 1913 obituary.

A Union soldier took the boy to Major Abram D. Sternberg, of the 186th New York Infantry, who took him under his protective wing. The boy "was the major's servant from that day until many years afterward." In one battle, the major's horse was shot from beneath him. According to the Freeman obituary, "The lad galloped into the thick of battle with another mount and transferred the saddle from the fallen horse to the fresh mount."

At war's end, the youth accompanied Major Sternberg to Washington and then to Reynolds Corners in the town of Clayton. He became a horse trainer in Sackets Harbor and Watertown, where he spent his later years as coachman for the A. Ten Eyck Lansing family.

When a laborer named Harry Gaines died in May 1909 in his home at 562 Morrison Street, he left in his tidy estate $500 for the purpose of building a new AME Zion Church. The YMCA, already a financial supporter of the church, assisted in acquiring a piece of land on Morrison Street, and work began rapidly for a new house of worship.

Church members raised more money, and they did most of the work themselves. They worked by lantern light, the *Times* reported in September 1909:

> *It was hard at times when the work needed to be rushed for the men who labored had the time only after the hours of their regular toil. Yet the work has been rushed through with remarkable promptitude and has reached a stage so that everything is ready for the ceremony of tomorrow. Late last night by the light of lanterns many members of the church were engaged in working on the church.*

On September 19, only four months after Harry Gaines provided the impetus, Bishop C.R. Harris of Salisbury, North Carolina, presided at the church dedication. Helping with the ceremony was the choir from Hope Presbyterian Church.

The congregation of Reverend Noah C. Rountree named the church for one of the trustees, Frank E. Thomas, who in his yard at 525 Water Street made every concrete block for the structure. A pattern maker for Bagley & Sewall Company, Watertown, Mr. Thomas was a native of Barnes Corners, born in 1856. He died in February 1932. One of his five brothers, Phineas, who was a farmer in Tylerville, was also among the church's builders.

Within five years, the church developed structural problems, particularly in the cellar, requiring renovations in 1914. "Just think of it," marveled Reverend Corel Campbell, pastor, following completion of repairs, "a month ago there was two feet of water in this cellar. And now look at it. In the winter the cellar was a regular pond and the children skated down there." Plumbing was updated, a porch added and a sidewalk built around the building. Even with that accomplished, the structure was only ten years old when another pastor, Reverend John R. Dickinson, was talking in February 1919 of selling it and finding a new location.

The minister, having just paid off the church's $500 debt in his seven months on the pulpit there, said that the parish's interests "will be greatly stimulated if the church is not so far removed from the center of the city," the *Times* reported. But such plans for this church of about twenty-five people never went beyond the talking stages.

The survival of Pastor George Barton Williams was labeled as nothing less than miraculous in the January 6, 1947 issue of the *Times*. Late on the preceding Saturday night, Reverend Williams grabbed his newspaper, walked out of his kitchen and settled down in the dining room of his parsonage attached to Thomas AME Zion Church. Within minutes, an explosion rocked the house. The minister had kindled a coal fire in his kitchen steam range but had forgotten to fill a hot-water pan in front of the stove with water, the fire department determined. When he discovered his error, he added cold water, generating excessive steam pressure.

The overheated appliance exploded, propelling hot coals and stove parts into the plaster ceiling and adjacent rooms. Furniture, linoleum and window curtains were ignited, four windows were shattered and the kitchen sink was ripped from the wall. City fire companies responding to the 11:14 p.m.

alarm doused flames in the living room, confining the blast's damage to two rooms and saving the church. Two members of the parish, Glenn E. DePuy and Robert Sinclair, boarded up exposed sections of the house, which only recently had been redecorated.

A community fund drive helped the small church recover from its uninsured loss. The membership then was probably about the same as it is today, between twenty-five and thirty.

Ora Hawkins, owner of More Than a Bagel on Public Square, has made the church her place of worship since she moved in 1962 from New Jersey to Watertown. In her years there, she said that she has seen the church hit desperate times, with attendance dipping to as low as two or three people. "But we had some very dedicated people, and we worked hard and sacrificed more to keep our church open," she said.

At one time in its history, more than two hundred worshipers filed into the little church's pews, according to its nonresident pastor, Reverend Baums, who commutes from Syracuse. He said that he leads a "very transitional" church with a membership of about twenty, mostly military, personnel. "We see changes in our people," he said, "but we're a family."

One descendant of the man for whom Thomas AME Zion Church was named still lives in Watertown and is a member of the church family. Henrietta Smith, wife of Andrew Smith, 615 East Main Street, is a daughter of the late Agnes Thomas Howard, who was a daughter of Frank E. Thomas.

Church records and a *Watertown Daily Times* obituary referred to the church benefactor as Henry Gaines. But the Watertown City Directory and Gaines's estate documents in Jefferson County Surrogate Court identified him as Harry.

Church member William "Buster" Crabb contributed to this section, and Times *librarians Patricia Delaney and Esther Daniels, as well as the Watertown City Clerk's Office, assisted in research.*

Soldiers' Executions Halted Thanks to North Man's Message to President Lincoln

Five Union soldiers, charged with desertion, stood minutes away from eternity when, suddenly, a courier arrived with word from President Abraham Lincoln. Orders were barked to the firing squad: their weapons could be relaxed. The episode in 1864 illustrated "the great kindness of heart of President Lincoln," said Jefferson D. Shultz, a Lewis County man who claimed partial responsibility for this reprieve.

When America remembered Lincoln's birthday eighty-two years ago, Mr. Shultz, a Civil War veteran living at Lyons Falls, told the story of how he got a message to the president about an impending injustice. He was serving as a Union prison guard, having already seen his share of battle since signing on with the Fifth New York Heavy Artillery at Sackets Harbor, New York. One of his prisoners told of going for an innocent stroll and having things end up terribly wrong.

"A young man enlisted to join my regiment, and while on the way with other recruits to join their regiments, they were waiting at Baltimore for connecting trains," Mr. Shultz told the *Watertown Daily Times* in February 1930. So, the young soldier took a walk to check out the town. That, it turned out, was not a wise thing to do. A provost guard tracked him down, and he was charged with desertion.

"At that time, desertions were quite frequent and punishment very severe," Mr. Shultz continued. "This young man was considered a deserter and with five others was sentenced to execution." Having heard the young man's sad tale, Shultz wanted to solicit the sympathy of Mr. Lincoln. But soldiers were not allowed to write to the president. "I secured the interest of a Catholic priest who frequently visited the prison, and he wrote President Lincoln," Mr. Shultz said.

The fateful day arrived. Five doomed men were marched out to their execution. As all the troops of the post watched, as required, the men were securely tied and blindfolded. They were then seated on coffins, situated in a line in front of the firing squad. Before the order was given to aim rifles, though, an orderly rushed up to the commanding officer with orders from Washington. President Lincoln had issued a reprieve. All five lives were spared that day, and a few days later, pardons were granted to four of the men.

"I had the pleasure of returning all but one to the regiments to which they belonged," Mr. Shultz said. "The exception was a man who had repeatedly deserted and re-enlisted to obtain bounties. That one I saw executed," he said.

Jefferson Shultz, son of Solomon and Phoebe Sisson Shultz, was born on June 18, 1844, in the town of Denmark. When he was three, he was separated from his parents because of his mother's health and lived in a Tug Hill area called Austin Settlement, in the town of Denmark.

With his eighteenth birthday two months behind him, Mr. Shultz responded to President Lincoln's call for enlistees to help preserve the Union. Following his August 3, 1862 enlistment—he signed on the dotted line in Copenhagen—he received his marching orders in Sackets Harbor and was sent in a battalion of six hundred men to Washington, where he glimpsed the president.

"Arriving at Washington and finding no light guns with which to equip them, they were transferred to the heavy artillery," he wrote about his company in 1934. "The 12 Jefferson County companies were made the 10th New York and the four from Lewis County made a battalion of the Fifth New York, two batteries of which were then in the field. Those men served partly in fortifications and later in infantry at the firing line."

Shultz served in the Shenandoah Valley of Virginia under Generals David Hunter, Franz Sigel and Philip H. Sheridan, participating in the 1864 campaign in which the Confederacy's position in western Virginia was broken. He saw combat at Harpers Ferry, Virginia; Cedar Creek at Martinsburg, Virginia; and Maryland Heights. He managed to get "only scared to death several times," he told a reporter.

Mr. Shultz was always reluctant to discuss his war service, the *Watertown Times* reported on his ninetieth birthday. It therefore remains a matter of conjecture whether he included himself when he wrote that a battery of men from Lowville "remained in service throughout the entire war and had the distinction of firing the last shot at Lee's surrender."

One memory he shared was of a day at the Washington Navy Yard when he said he was allowed to board and inspect the USS *Monitor*, one of the two ironclad vessels that battled to a draw in a historic encounter on March 9, 1862, at Hampton Roads, Virginia. He said he saw the "scars" that the craft sustained. "Those were dark days for the Union," he said. "We had lost many battles and each new commander seemed to make more errors than the former one."

Jefferson Shultz officially put his soldiering career behind him on July 6, 1865, when he was discharged at Sackets Harbor. Back home in Lewis County, he made education a priority, enrolling in school in Lowville. Later that year, he passed a full regents examination. He spent the next forty-three years working on railroads, beginning as one of the builders of the Utica and Black River Railroad.

"He is one of the men who built the railroads which tie the hamlet to the city, state to state and the whole country into an economic unit," said one of his admirers, John Cox Jr., in 1932. "He was a man who did not watch with undue eagerness the slow moving office clock to announce quitting time, but a man who made the most of his opportunities and performed his work faithfully; worked overtime if necessary and raised himself to the limit of his ability."

With construction of the line closing a link from Boonville to Lowville in 1869, he took a break on January 26 to marry Helen Upright of Lyons Falls. 'Til death did they part, as his wife died forty years later.

Three months into wedlock, Mr. Shultz was off to a new job as assistant engineer of construction with the New Haven, Middletown and Willimantic Railroad. That kept him occupied until 1875, when he was laying out plans for tracks running from Brooklyn to Orient Point. The proposed run was scrubbed by an economic depression, as was his job. He took what jobs he could get, sticking with railroad work. He went back to where he started, the Utica and Black River Railroad, toiling as a brakeman, a baggage man and then a conductor.

A recovering economy in 1881 returned him to the service he had mastered. He was given charge of construction of the New York, West Shore and Buffalo line in Herkimer County. The accomplishment about which he boasted most occurred in Wayne County, where he supervised the laying of tracks across the Montezuma marshes and the Savannah sinkhole.

"On a theory of his own, Mr. Shultz drove the 20 spans of 54 feet each in the Montezuma marsh," the *Times* reported in 1932. "Foundation piles varying in depth from 30 to 70 feet were driven to distribute better the load. The bridge has remained as built for over 45 years."

As one project concluded, he was riding the rails to another. The Tioga Railroad in Pennsylvania hired him in 1884 to supervise straightening and improvement of its tracks. One year later, the Erie Railroad having taken over the Tioga, he was appointed "roadmaster" for lines serving coal mines.

After being granted a summer rest in the Adirondacks due to illness in 1890, he was back on the job for Erie, directing construction of a twenty-mile run along with a terminal, a warehouse and a coal shipping trestle. Next he was on the payroll of the New York Central and Hudson River Railroad Company, being named in 1892 general roadmaster of the Rome, Watertown and Ogdensburg division. Mr. Shultz capped his railroad career with appointment to the steam railroad commission in 1898. A few months after his wife died in 1909, he retired.

Fishing was his hobby, and Mr. Shultz and a buddy he hadn't seen for three decades came up with a whopper of a fish tale when they enjoyed a reunion at Lyons Falls. The occasion was the railroad man's ninetieth birthday, and his visitor, Charles E. Palmiter, had come from Watertown. Their account of a fishing excursion that occurred forty years earlier, when they were giving railroad executives a tour of Benson Mines, appeared on June 22, 1934, in the *Times*:

> *Reaching Mooers, the party went in to Little Pesuite where Mr. Shultz had the only boat on the lake hidden, but by the time they were ready to use it the officials had discovered the hiding place and had debarked with the vessel, leaving Shultz and Palmiter behind.*
>
> *Determined to fish, the two men finally discovered an old dilapidated water-soaked raft which soon became awash when it was boarded. This was not enough to stop real fishermen, however, and the casting for trout began.*
>
> *All of a sudden the cry "overboard" emanated from the throat of Jefferson Shultz, and Mr. Palmiter, too excited to inquire, leaped into the water.*

"The fish are sinking the raft," replied Mr. Shultz in answer to Mr. Palmiter's inquiry.

So the two fishermen, with mind on nothing but keeping their prize catch, swam about three rods to shore pushing the raft ahead of them. On shore it was discovered that in less than two hours, two 20-pound creels had been crammed with speckled trout.

Jefferson Shultz died at ninety-two on October 30, 1936. He had no children.

Times *librarian Esther Daniels found this story.*

A Soldier's Heart Turns Homeward

Edwards Man's Letters Offer Personal Account of Civil War

Victory was surely just around the corner, or so wrote a Union soldier from Edwards.

Horace Barnes, finding himself on the fringe of battle, promised his family a timely return to plant the crops on his farm. But the forty-six-year-old volunteer in arms was making a promise that he could not fulfill. After all, this was the winter of 1861–62. The War Between the States had a long, bloody path ahead. For Mr. Barnes, it would be a short path—a dead end.

Today, 137 years later, the quiet St. Lawrence County village of Edwards, with its 440 residents, takes pride looking back to the days before its talc mines were abandoned and it was sideswiped by Route 58. Part of that pride lies in the men who sacrificed their lives for their country.

The Civil War prompted Thomas Ivers, Harvey Winslow, Orvil Morris, Henry and Isaac King, Mr. Lindsey and Mr. Beach and his son, to name a few, to leave their loved ones and abandon their fields. And then there was Horace Barnes, father of six, who left not only a farm but also management of the Rushton House, a hotel on Main Street. We know a bit about Horace because of his letters home, preserved by his family and now in the hands of his great-grandson, Edwards resident Earl B. Noble, and the Edwards History Center.

It was in October 1861 that Mr. Barnes parted from his familiar surroundings. Certainly he was no green kid looking for adventure, but still, he seemed to welcome this interruption in his life. "I can't say that I am sorry

Left: Horace Barnes wrote home to Edwards, New York, promising to return from the battle front. Illness shattered his promise. *Courtesy LaVerne Freeman and the Edwards History Center.*

Below: Barnes's Rushton House hotel, shown in 1866. *Courtesy LaVerne Freeman and the Edwards History Center.*

I enlisted," wrote the recruit in Albany on November 23, 1861, to his wife, Ellison. "I think [I] have enjoyed myself about as well as I have for some time past." And his hiatus from the hotel seemed welcome. "When I was at home my business matters made me almost crazy," he said in that first letter.

He showed a naïveté about what lay ahead. "The prospect now is we shall be home before we shall ever have a chance to see a fight," he said. But make no mistake, Horace believed in the cause for which he joined the Ninth Regiment of the New York Volunteer Cavalry. "If this regiment should be disbanded I should not feel satisfied unless the Union was restored and the Stars and Stripes be furled over every State in America," he wrote on January 6, 1862. The regiment was new, hardly ready for battle in 1861. Its first assignment was Washington, D.C.

Horace Barnes's letters are full of news about his life as a soldier, but they also show a continual longing for home and family. Following, in part, is how Horace, who had been a teacher, reported from his quarters, in his words and spellings.

December 1, 1861—"General McLellan went across the Potomac on Thursday with 41 thousand soldiers On Friday the day we got here there was pitched battle with the Rebbles. We could hear the guns very distinctly from Washington. The particulars of the battle we have not heard…

"We are to be the Flag Company. I have no idea that we shall ever see a battle for I think the war will be over with before we shall be fit for service."

December 11, 1861—"I enjoy good health. Nearly half of our company is sick with the measels…We still are in suspense about this rigament. Our officers are as much in suspense as we are ourselves. As for me I enlisted because I thought our government wanted me but if they do not it's just as well although I should be glad if they would decide the matter…

"We drill about 5 hours in each day and the rest of the time we are cooking, doing our washing and ironing and cooking our meals…I may not come home till spring."

January 6, 1862 (written from Camp Fenton)—"I feel affraid sometimes that I might fall prey to disease. That is the only fears that I have now…

"Boys [to his sons] I wish you both could be here once so then you could better understand what I write. You would see more than you will in all your lives if you always stay in Edwards. After all there is no place like home and they are the best off who stay there…

"How do you git along for wood? Do you take good care of the cows? Ma never wrote to me about the house whether she got the house fixed so as to be comfortable. Did you get the doors made and the windows in? Have you got hay enough to winter the cows?…

"There was in this company yesterday 26 excused by the surgeon as being onfit for duty and many of them in their beds. But there is onely one in our company I consider dangerous a dying most every day. But I think on the whole that the health of the regiment is improving."

February 17, 1862—"I hope Ellison you will not get discouraged about my being gone from home for as things now look it will be a short duration for I think the war will be brought to a speedy close as our armies are now moving forward with great success. I have no doubt but what the war will be over in three months…when this is done I shall be satisfied to return to my family and think that I have done my duty…

"Ellison I have no doubt but what I shall be home by the first of July if not before."

March 2, 1862—"I think this month and next will about tell the story with the war…We probably shall be sent somewhere for guards, perhaps to the City as I understand that those that were there have been ordered to moove. I do not want you to flatter yourself to much that I am coming home very soon for it is all an uncertainty about how things may turn."

March 19, 1862 (now in Alexandria, Virginia)—"We left Camp Fenton last Saturday and come to this place with the expectations of onely staying here over night but when we got here the army was not ready to moove as there was not vessels enough to take us all at once…There has been since last Saturday 75,000 troops arrived at this place to be sent somewhere… Our regiment will be about the last to leave as our regiment has the honor of goeing as an escort for the army and take charge of the aminitions…Our regiment is quartered in the fields. We have taken nothing with us but our haversacks, canteens and one blanket a piece."

March 24, 1862 (at Camp Elsworth, near Alexandria)—"I would say that a soldier's life is a life of suspense not knowing one day what we are goeing to do the next…Our regiment was detailed as an escort for the amenition train consequently we shall have to wait till the last…We are here in camp near Alexandria without tents. We have to seek our lodging in some old buildings which has made quite comfortable untill today…

"We have just rec'd orders that not a man to leave the grounds…I am learning how to take care of myself pretty well which I find is indispensably necessary for our head officers care very little for the welfare of their men. They are affraid that if we git good quarters at night that we shall enjoy ourselves to well and there won't be as many be likely to die off by disease…I have to write this letter on my lap sitting on a bag of oats on a rinkled up dirty sheet of paper which makes a horrible looking letter."

April 4, 1862 (at Fortress Monroe)—"The army is mooving forward and we are in hopes of soon being able to achieve a glorious victory…There is 180 thousand men a head of me and the roads are crowded full all of the while, night and day…

"This is beautiful country but such a destruction of buildings, fences, gardens, fruit trees, and everything else it really makes me feel bad…Trees are all leaving out. It makes me sick of that cold country and if my family was here I think I could content myself to stay here the remainder of days…

"Do not give yourselves any trouble about me. As long as my health is good I can endure any other privation that we have to encounter."

April 8, 1862—"We are…a few miles from Yorktown where they are having a big fight and when that is over we probably shall go with our escort to Yorktown and from there to Richmond which will be the amont of time that we are detailed on this escort and then we are agoeing to be mustered out of the service. I shall be home the first part of May if nothing happens."

April 12, 1862—"There is a big fight goeing on at Yorktown a few miles from us…After Yorktown is taken and our forces are in order again then the 9th Cavalry will go back to Washington and be mustered out of service.… There is goeing to be an awful fight…General McLellan is in the field with his men and we don't expect anything else but a glorious victory…

"If I come home I think I shall be there in time to plant some corn and potatoes."

April 27, 1862 (at Camp Winfield Scott near Yorktown, Virginia)—"When I wrote you from Fortress Monroe I then thought…we should be mustered out of the service, but things moove very slow. While I am writing I can hear the cannons roar…We never shall git our discharge untill the fight is over with…Although we are in the advance of the right wing of the army still our position is not a very dangerous one as all the business we doe is guard duty…Our regiment is in about 2 1/2 miles from Yorktown where we shall see the hardest part of the fight."

May 11, 1862 (a week after McClellan occupied Yorktown)—"I embrace this oppertunity of writing to let you know that I am still in the land of the living and in the enjoyment of very good health…I wrote that we probably should come home after the Siege of Yorktown but we are now 35 miles above Yorktown on York River…on the very ground where we had a hard fight a few days ago…

"We now expect to go from here to Richmond which I persume will be as far as we shall go south. There is an order isshued for the 9th NY Cavalry to be mustered out of the service but the order has been suspended and we… shall continue to go as escort for the amnition train to Richmond…You need not look for me home before the first of July…

"If you have received my letters give yourself no uneasyness about our gitting killed in battle, but there is a good deal of danger of sickness. There is a great many sick in the army…

"General McLellan has just rode by with his bodyguard amid the cheers of some ten thousand troops. He rode through the amass crowd with his hat off waveing his hand as a welcome to his soldiers. He has just got off his horse in site of our tent. We probably shall know soon what the orders to be."

That is the last known letter from Horace Barnes.

In a letter dated June 1, 1862, written at the soldier's bedside, another soldier informed Mrs. Barnes that Horace was "unwell" but "he is now doing well, and a fair prospect continuing so."

Then came a telegram from Washington, D.C., dated June 6, 1862. It said, in part, "Barnes has died this day and if the family wants his body embalmed, telegraph." He was suffering from a fever when he died in an improvised hospital in the patent office in Washington. He was buried at Arlington Cemetery.

Horace Barnes was among 110 members of the Ninth Regiment who died from disease. Had he remained healthy, he might have found his way to Gettysburg, where the regiment stood proud defending a battle line. "Suffice it to say that the enemy poured their veteran columns against our line of dismounted men, who stood like a wall of fire and repulsed their repeated charges for two mortal hours," said Lieutenant Colonel Wilber G. Bentley at a July 1, 1888 dedication of the regiment's monument on the battlefield. The quote is taken from *New York at Gettysburg*, published in 1900 by the James B. Lyon Company, Albany.

Ellison Barnes survived her husband by twenty-six years, dying eight months after her sixty-second birthday. Of the five girls (one died before the war at age eleven) and two boys fathered by Horace Barnes, Emily Eldora Barnes Beach was the last to survive. She died in February 1935, only thirteen days shy of her eighty-first birthday. Earl Noble's mother, Addie Barnes Noble, was a daughter of Earl Barnes, the soldier's older son.

The town of Edwards saw 130 of its men leave for the Civil War. Among the approximately 94 who came home was Thomas Ivers, who served the North as a spy behind Confederate lines. A prisoner exchange spared him from an October 1862 death sentence ordered by General Robert E. Lee, according to Edwards deputy historian LaVerne Freeman.

An Irish immigrant, Mr. Ivers died at age fifty-one in 1869, leaving his wife, Mary Ann, and four children, ages twelve to nineteen. By 1880, his family had left Edwards.

The hotel that Horace Barnes managed was one of thirty-four buildings destroyed in a July 4, 1894 fire sparked not by holiday fireworks but by a windswept chimney fire. The edifice was replaced by the Thomas House, later called Hotel Edwards, which burned down in May 1970. The location is now a vacant lot.

Theresa's Schule Bell

A Civil War Southerner Given New Life in the North

The train's shrill whistle alerted the small gathering at the Philadelphia, New York station to the anticipated arrival of yet another coffin from a Civil War front. After the squeal of steel on steel brought the "iron horse" to its gradual halt, and after the engine's gasp of steam had been exhausted on this April day in 1865, an honor guard began to remove the wooden box from one of the train's cars. A member of the waiting party from Theresa signed documents to claim the remains of a fallen soldier, Schule Bell. Shedding tears, the mourners watched while Bell's box was positioned on a horse-drawn wagon. Then the procession solemnly filed away, en route to Schule's home in Theresa for family viewing.

A while later, safely out of sight of the military escort, an air of excitement dried the fake tears as some "family members" scurried to pry free the coffin's cover. And there in the box was, as anticipated, a bell for the new "schule" (school), courtesy of Union soldiers' conspiracy against one of the Confederacy's locomotives.

Some hometown soldiers who were helping bring down the rebellion had learned that the village of Theresa could not afford to buy a bell for the new schoolhouse, so they concocted a scheme to perform their civic duty, Yankee-style.

The story, as retold in the 1992 book *Whispers From the Past* by Harold I. Sanderson of Carthage, New York, brings us to Petersburg, Virginia. The men in Union blue were aware of a train engine that had become partially submerged

"Schule Bell" remains on display at the Theresa, New York Primary School, which provided this photo.

in the James River. An eighty-pound bronze bell mounted on the locomotive would toll well for the new school back home, they thought. So—in the darkness of night, we suspect—the trio snatched their trophy. Having rung up that task, their next mission was to get it home. It so happened that one of the rebellious trio was a mortician's assistant. What better way to conceal this pilfered piece of Rebel property than in a coffin, he suggested.

Making sure that the body-length carton weighed about 140 pounds to match the average soldier, they planted a four-foot log and the bell on a mattress of straw in the coffin. They wrapped soldiers' apparel around the precious cargo, making sure that the bell's clapper was removed and separately cushioned lest some clatter awaken and frighten one of the men escorting the "body."

Proper documents were drawn up for this battle casualty, Schule Bell. In the meantime, letters were hustled off to loved ones back in Theresa, advising of the so-named soldier's sad demise and of his last ride to his final rest. According to Sanderson, the remains of Schule Bell were placed on a train the night of April 7, 1865, and were soon heading to the north woods.

Of course, some profit had to be made from this adventure. The school district purchased the bell for fifty dollars, according to a pre-1934 writing of Dr. Jeremiah R. Sturtevant. When the new two-story school building constructed of Potsdam sandstone opened in 1869, pupils responded to the clanging of the Confederate bell.

The names of the conspiring trio are undisclosed in the Sanderson account. However, one name, Otis Brooks, has survived the passage of time, according to Dr. Sturtevant's notation and *The History of Theresa*, a group effort in 1980 edited by Ronald E. Sinclair.

But still another name surfaces. August Kissell was a Union soldier, and he, too, went south to fight. But all that is known for sure is that as a dealer in monuments, he made sure that Schule Bell received due remembrance in the local cemetery. Upon a simple stone he chiseled "Schule Bell 1865."

Otis Brooks was indeed in the vicinity of where Schule Bell was taken captive. Having enlisted at age twenty-nine in August 1862 with the Tenth New York Heavy Artillery, he saw action in the Battle of Petersburg and along the James River, according to the *Genealogical and Family History of the County of Jefferson*, published by Rensselaer A. Oakes. He returned home unscathed and was discharged in June 1865.

Otis Brooks took up house building in Oswego but soon was closer to home, building businesses. He operated a sawmill for six years along the Antwerp-Wilna town line and then sold out in favor of erecting a gristmill in West Carthage. Another gristmill awaited his operation in Philadelphia, where he subsequently built two sawmills. Finally, he purchased a share of a lumberyard at Philadelphia and opened a woodworking shop at Clayton, laying the foundation for the Otis Brooks Lumber Company of Philadelphia, which would long survive his passing in April 1909.

"Here the proprietor is found during the week, not only superintending the work, but often bearing a hand anywhere that it seems to be needed," his contemporary, Mr. Oakes, wrote. "It will be seen that he is energetic and industrious, and blessed with sound executive ability. Together with his men, he takes his breakfast at six o'clock in the morning, and with them proceeds about the work of the day. He is respected and admired by all who know him, for his straightforward, manly qualities, his diligence in business, and upright treatment of all with whom he comes in contact."

As for August Kissell, the stories about him are truly monumental. He was born on June 18, 1847, in Germany. At fifteen, he sailed to America.

Penniless and speaking no English, he joined family members in Theresa. His brother, Peter, put him to work at the trade that would shape his future: stonemasonry. At the age of nineteen, he was an enlisted man, ready to fight for Mr. Lincoln's army under the colors of the Ninety-fourth New York Volunteer Infantry Regiment, which trained at Sackets Harbor. He wasn't even at a battle front yet when, in March 1862, he experienced an unexpected peril of war. The unit's train plunged into the Hudson River near Poughkeepsie. About twenty soldiers drowned, but obviously Mr. Kissell was not among them.

The German advanced from one battlefield to another, seeing Americans' blood spilled at Cedar Mountain, Bull Run, Thoroughfare Gap, Fredericksburg, Chancellorsville and Gettysburg. Moving on under the command of General Ulysses S. Grant, he spent his twenty-second birthday in combat near Petersburg. But there ends any likelihood of his involvement in the capture of Schule Bell, for he himself was captured.

The Confederates moved him from one stockade to another before finally placing him with some eleven thousand prisoners at Salisbury, North Carolina. There, survival depended on a daily ration of four ounces of cornmeal bread, according to an interview Mr. Kissell gave in 1905 to a *Syracuse Herald* reporter. After an escape attempt was quashed in November 1864, Mr. Kissell and his comrades were denied their bread for two days, with the stockade commander trying to induce them into pledging allegiance to the Confederacy. "Death before dishonor!" the men shouted in defiance.

In the two months that followed, some of the Union men, Kissell included, managed to build up a trade with a few of their Rebel guards, who lined their pockets with Yankee cash and bulged their cheeks with chewing tobacco, for which they paid the captives Rebel cash. Finally, some Union boys had enough Confederate currency to bribe one of their guards, Albert Childers, into arranging an escape.

Mr. Kissell's ticket to freedom cost $300. On the night of January 27, 1865, August Kissell and six companions, disguised as guards, walked out of the camp.

For days they subsisted on raw corn and wandered through swamps and icy waters to throw off the bloodhounds that tracked them. Seventeen days and 150 miles later, with the party of seven now separated, Mr. Kissell and a single companion trudged through four inches of snow to a cabin in Iredell County, North Carolina. While the other soldier watched from afar, the freezing and hungry New Yorker knocked at the modest structure's door, figuring that he had no choice but to be honest as he begged for shelter. Identifying himself as an escaped Union soldier, Mr. Kissell pleaded to an old man in the cabin, "I ask you, in the name of God, to assist and protect me."

Asked for proof of his claim, the visitor opened his overcoat to display a ragged blue uniform and a belt buckle bearing the U.S. emblem. The old man and his daughter responded to Kissell, who then advised them of his friend outdoors. Fortunately, the two fugitives had found Union sympathizers. After being fed and housed that night, the men prepared at midnight to resume their northward trek. But they hardly knew where to go.

The young woman, Sina Myers, volunteered to lead them a short way to get them moving toward the Blue Ridge Mountains and the Tennessee border. Riding a horse from the family's stable, she took one man at a time across a creek. Mr. Kissell was her second rider.

She led them to a road to Jonesborough and then bade them farewell. Miss Myers, her clothing frozen stiff, struggled with chattering teeth as she issued a warning. "Soldier," she addressed Kissell, "there are a thousand chances against you, but if you are surrounded, fight as long as you've a drop of blood left, for it'll be easier for them to shoot you than to guard you back to Salisbury."

As the escapees tackled the mountains, they found another sympathetic household. And there to the rescue came, to their surprise, a Confederate soldier. Mr. Kissell told the *Watertown Daily Times* in 1916 about this next experience in his search for home. William Byrd was actually a deserter, and he hoped to join the Union army. There were search parties nearby, he cautioned, and he led his acquaintances to a log corn house, where he told them to dig through the corn. Four to six feet down, they uncovered a large box in which they were instructed to hide.

Trusting this man, Kissell and his companion, a Pennsylvanian, complied. A cover was placed above them, and then they heard corn being deposited on the box. They must have feared that this might be their coffin as they closed their eyes and went to sleep. A few hours later, a breath of fresh air greeted them as Mr. Byrd opened their hideout. A search party had passed by, he reported, and the corn house grave had probably saved them. The turncoat accompanied them the rest of the way until, on March 2, 1865, they reached Union lines at Knoxville, Tennessee. Mr. Kissell was now safe, and Mr. Byrd was signing up to fight for the Union.

August Kissell never forgot. He planned to find his rescuers. Around the turn of the century, he wrote to newspaper editors seeking help but got nothing in return. Then he mailed vaguely addressed envelopes, seeking family members who might be able to lead him to William Byrd and Sina Myers.

Finally, steered by various connections he had made, he sent a letter early in 1902 to a W.C. Myers in Osbornville, North Carolina. A reply came in March. The correspondent said that Sina was his aunt and that August could still find her in Iredell County, under the name Sina Summers.

On an evening in October 1902, August Kissell and Sina Summers sat together at her home reminiscing about their brief wartime acquaintanceship and sharing stories about the years that had followed. But his search was not finished. A letter he sent in 1916 to "William Byrd or to any of his relatives" reached the old soldier's hands and earned a happy reply. The veterans, too old to travel, had to entrust their exchange of life stories to the postal service.

Mr. Kissell took his remembrances further, taking advantage of his work as a monument dealer. In Theresa's Oakwood Cemetery, he placed a prominent monument memorializing and naming fifty-eight Northern New York men who fought in the Revolutionary War, the War of 1812 and the Civil War. Also on the monument, he listed three "female heroes"—the first, of course, being Sina Summers of Hunter Creek, North Carolina. Also named were two women in Gettysburg, Jennie Wait and Jennie Topton.

Civil War monument at Oakwood Cemetery, Theresa, New York. *Courtesy* Watertown Daily Times.

On the monument, erected in 1910, is this epitaph:

> *Passenger, if thou art a friend of a soldier,*
> *drop a tear over the dust of all heroes.*
> *For us their precious lives they gave*
> *for freedom's sacred cause they died.*
> *And toiled by day in hunger, head and cold,*
> *and lay at night wrapped in the chilly fold*
> *of stormy skies and tempest wild*
> *without a whispered cheer.*
> *Legend may fade from the portal,*
> *keystone and column may crumble and fall.*
> *They were the builders whose work is immortal,*
> *crowned with the Dome that is over us all.*

Mr. Kissell also had a prominent monument awaiting his burial. He died on March 28, 1923. He was survived by a son, Abner Kissell, and a daughter, Mabel Westcott, but there are no known direct descendants.

Otis Brooks, whose wife was named Celestia, left a son, Frank H., and a daughter, Allie Brooks. Frank's son, William, had a daughter, Mary Brooks-Mercier, who made her home in Clayton, New York. She died in 2007.

Otis Brooks is credited with a role in bringing a Southern bell home to Theresa, New York. *Courtesy* Watertown Daily Times.

As for Schule Bell, "For nearly 70 years it summoned to school, to worship, to fires, and even to Halloween Eve pranks," wrote Dr. Sturtevant on the document that today rests beside the bell in a display cabinet in the Theresa Elementary School. It was retired in 1939. The Schule Bell monument at Oakwood Cemetery has disappeared.

Dr. Sturtevant was a medical doctor and optician for many years in Theresa, and he served on the village school board. He boasted that when he first came to Theresa, on February 3, 1873, he rode in on the very first regular train to arrive in the village. He was eighty-six when he died on January 19, 1934.

My thanks for their assistance with this section go to Harold Sanderson, Times *librarian Esther Daniels and Eleanor Love Ebbighausen of Watertown, who has studied the August Kissell genealogy because her former husband was an indirect descendant.*

Bradley Winslow, Civil War Hero

Business places in Watertown, New York, closed their doors for the afternoon, while members of military and patriotic organizations turned out for a "most imposing military funeral," as the *Watertown Daily Times* described the community's farewell to an old soldier and statesman.

That morning, October 27, 1914, as flags on public buildings were lowered to half-staff, the body of General Bradley Winslow was taken into the drill hall of the armory on Arsenal Street to lie in state for a few hours. Then came the procession to Trinity Episcopal Church. As a horse-drawn hearse bearing the general's flag-draped coffin slowly marked its path to the church, men of the National Guard, the Naval Militia, the general's colleagues from Joe Spratt Post, Grand Army of the Republic (GAR), the sons of Veterans Camp named for the late general and the Daughters of the American Revolution followed in a solemn march. At the conclusion of a service conducted by Reverend Francis W. Eason, rector, the final march for General Winslow found its way to Brookside Cemetery.

Bradley Winslow, boasting of ancestry to Edward Winslow, a *Mayflower* pilgrim who became governor of Plymouth Colony, was born on August 1, 1831, in the town of Watertown. After being educated in local schools and in seminaries at Cazenovia and Fulton in New York State and Kingston, Pennsylvania, he chose to follow a career in law, beginning in 1852 as an assistant to Judge James F. Starbuck in Watertown. He went to Poughkeepsie Law School, and in 1855, he was admitted to the practice of law.

Four years later, voters in Jefferson County elected him district attorney, but it was a post he would abandon in 1861 when he answered the call of national duty. The "Jefferson County regiment," officially the Thirty-fifth Regiment of the New York Volunteer Infantry, was formed that year, and Winslow was named a captain. Soon he was elevated to lieutenant colonel and was a leader in combat against Confederate forces at Manassas Junction, Fredericksburg, the Second Battle of Bull Run, Chantilly, South Mountain and Antietam.

His personal fight to preserve the Union appeared over in December 1862, when illness forced him to resign. But he won the battle against his health, and late in the summer of 1864, he gathered recruits from Jefferson, Lewis and Herkimer Counties to build eight companies of the 186th Regiment, New York Volunteer Infantry. Within a month of his return, he was in combat and was on his way to becoming a near-witness to the collapse of the Confederacy.

A camp of New York's Thirty-fifth Volunteers, Jefferson County Regiment. *Courtesy Library of Congress.*

As the Union army carried out a siege of Petersburg in southern Virginia, Colonel Winslow led his regiment on April 2, 1865, in a bayonet charge on Fort Mahone in the last campaign before Richmond. During what was called "a gallant charge," the colonel was shot in the abdomen. He narrowly escaped death. On April 9, 1865, only six days before his assassination, President Abraham Lincoln cited Colonel Winslow for "gallant and meritorious conduct" and conferred on him the honor of brevet brigadier general.

With peace restored to the nation, General Winslow declined an offered position in the army and returned to Jefferson County, but he later accepted appointment as brigadier general of the New York National Guard. General Winslow reentered the political theater at war's end, immediately winning back his position as district attorney. Subsequent elections brought the Republican to the mayor's seat in Watertown in 1875 and to the New York Senate in 1879.

But his allegiance to his fellow men at arms held strong. He was a charter member of the state's department of the Grand Army of the Republic and served as the state unit's first junior vice commander. At the GAR national convention in 1899, he nominated a Watertown man for the post of national commander and then served the new commander, Colonel Albert D. Shaw, as aide-de-camp. Colonel Shaw had fought with Winslow in the old Thirty-fifth Volunteers.

A newspaper even suggested that Winslow went down fighting for his comrades. In 1914, a proposal was presented to the voters in Jefferson County to erect a building memorializing those men who fought in the Civil War. "It was the one object of his later years to which he devoted himself and in his feeble old age, when he ought to have been sparing himself," the *Watertown Daily Times* editorialized. "He worked incessantly for the accomplishment of this purpose and broke himself down so that he became an easy prey to pneumonia. There is no doubt whatever that he gave his life that his comrades of the Civil War should be remembered."

The editorial, appearing on October 26, 1914, the day after the eighty-three-year-old soldier's death, advocated "another reason" for acceptance of the measure: "It becomes a memorial to him also."

Watertown voters concurred with the sentiment, giving the nod for a $100,000 expenditure by the county. Their counterparts in the rest of the county were less receptive, however, and the bid was rejected on November 3, 1914, by a margin of little more than one thousand votes.

(Seven Isles,) ALEXANDRIA BAY, N. Y., June 1, 1902.

To the Public:

General and Mrs. Bradley Winslow will open their beautiful St. Lawrence River property, known as Seven Isles, for the entertainment of a limited number of guests. It is a charming place, a group of islands composed of three islands and four smaller ones lying contiguous and connected by foot bridges. They are situate directly on the steamboat channel in American waters about one mile and one-quarter up stream from Alexandria Bay, and are covered with beautiful trees affording abundant shade. It is an ideal place especially for families, the surrounding waters near the shores are shallow and therefore quite safe for children.

There are cottages which a family or party of friends may occupy and enjoy the comforts and quiet of a home.

Application will at once be made to secure a postoffice

All steamers making the island rambles will stop at the dock belonging to the property.

A table d hote; excellent cuisene.

The grounds are ample affording opportunity for exercise and recreation. Lawn Tennis and other games may be indulged in.

Fine fishing in waters immediately adjacent.

No mosqnitoes.

Birds are numerous.

The natural beauty of the scenery we seek to preserve as far as possible A panorama of steamboats and other craft is constantly passing, usually within hailing distance.

Board by the day or week on reasonable terms.

Postoffice address until a new postoffice shall be established, Alexandria Bay, N. Y.

MR. AND MRS. BRADLEY WINSOW.

Letter from Bradley Winslow from his summer home on the St. Lawrence River. *Courtesy Jefferson County Historical Society.*

General Winslow was married twice. By his marriage to Geraldine M. Cooper, there was a son, John C. Winslow, who died before his parents, and two daughters, Charlotte Winslow Johnston and Florence Winslow Upham. He remarried in 1901. Poppie Holmes Burdick Winslow survived her husband and was sixty-eight when she died on Christmas Day 1928.

This section appeared in the fall 2001 issue of the Jefferson County Historical Society's Bulletin *and is reprinted here with the society's permission.*

Union Veterans Group Saw All Its Old Soldiers Fade Away

War stories bounced off the walls as ten old men socialized on a mild July afternoon in West Carthage, New York, more than eight decades ago. The nine guests were visiting Dr. George D. Hewitt, 25 Bridge Street, on the occasion of his eighty-ninth birthday. But put ten Civil War veterans averaging eighty-two years of age under one roof, and surely tales from Antietam, Fredericksburg, Petersburg, Chancellorsville and Appomattox would fill the air.

At least four of these men shared an even stronger bond. Dr. Hewitt Armand Hubbard, who just a day earlier had observed his eighty-first birthday; seventy-eight-year-old Jehu F. Osborn; and Lyle B. Bence, ninety, who would die three months later, had all battled under the colors of the 186th New York Volunteer Infantry, commanded by Watertown's Colonel Bradley Winslow. George Christman, about to turn eighty-two in another month, may have talked of seeing blood spilled in at least ten conflicts, including one of the battles at Bull Run. His turn came at Petersburg, with a wound to his left arm. Perhaps his battlefield physician was Dr. Hewitt, who had been pulled aside to be assistant sergeant in the medical department. "This shift never really interfered with the real business of fighting," Dr. Hewitt often commented. A participant in several exchanges with the enemy from the South, the doctor never suffered a scratch, he boasted.

Meanwhile, J. Mills Corwin, eighty-two, a Pennsylvania-born Union soldier who brought his tanning trade to Carthage back in 1897, could

John Hunter and Samuel VanPelt, Jefferson County's last surviving resident veterans of the Civil War. *Courtesy* Watertown Daily Times.

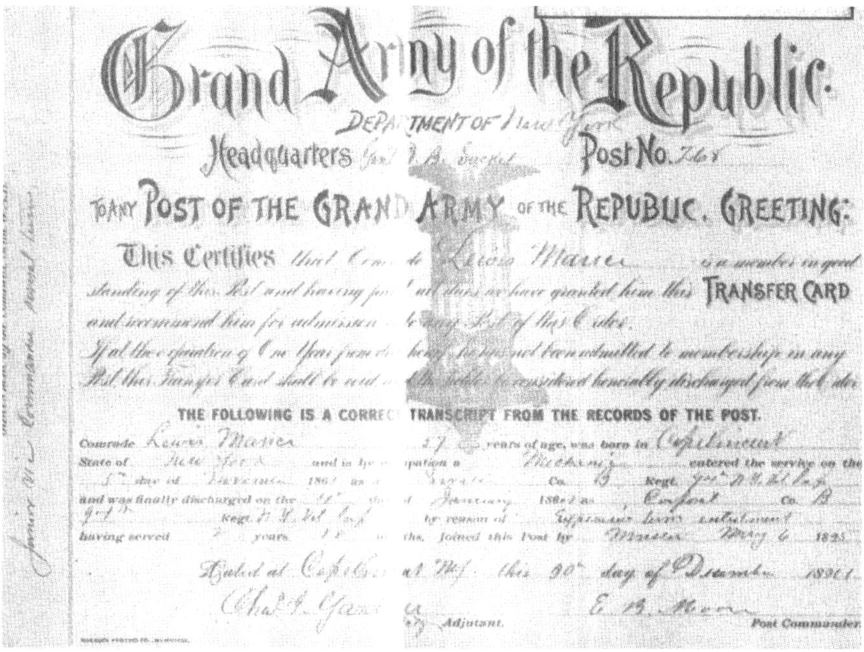

Grand Army of the Republic

DEPARTMENT OF New York

Headquarters ... Post No. 768

TO ANY POST OF THE GRAND ARMY OF THE REPUBLIC, GREETING:

This Certifies that Comrade Lewis Marie is a member in good standing of this Post and having paid all dues we have granted him this TRANSFER CARD and recommend him for admission to any Post of this Order.

If at the expiration of One Year from date hereof he has not been admitted to membership in any Post this Transfer Card shall be void and the holder be considered honorably discharged from the Order.

THE FOLLOWING IS A CORRECT TRANSCRIPT FROM THE RECORDS OF THE POST.

Comrade Lewis Marie ... years of age, was born in ... State of New York ... and in [illegible] occupation a Mechanic ... entered the service on the ... day of ... 186 ... as ... Co. ... Regt. ... and was finally discharged on the ... day of ... 186 ... as ... Co. ... Regt. ... by reason of ... having served ... years ... months ... days. Joined this Post by ... May 6 1885

Dated at ... this 30th day of December 1886

... Adjutant.

E. B. ... Post Commander.

Membership certificate of the Grand Army of the Republic, Joe Spratt Post of Watertown, New York. *Courtesy Jefferson County Historical Society.*

pipe in that he was at Antietam and Fredericksburg, too, with the Fifty-second Pennsylvania Regiment. And he might have described witnessing the surrender of General Robert E. Lee at Appomattox, as well as the three times he saw President Abraham Lincoln.

Rounding out this cast of warriors, who feasted on chicken pie dinner, were Patrick Finley, seventy-nine; William O'Horo, seventy-seven; Charles P. Walker, eighty-three; and F. Lansing Rockwood, seventy-nine. Mr. Hubbard, who had operated a livery stable and a hotel in his prime, was the last of this elite group to breathe words of the days when blue battled gray. He was ninety when he died on February 6, 1936. These ten men were survivors, members of the Grand Army of the Republic.

Fewer than 300,000 veterans of the army that was built to preserve the Union were still alive in August 1900 when a Watertown man, Albert D. Shaw, stood at a podium in Chicago as national commander of their fraternity, the Grand Army of the Republic. "The future of the organization can have but one issue, that of final historic ending by the death of its last surviving member," wrote Mr. Shaw, soldier turned international diplomat, for the GAR national convention program. The passing of the last surviving Union soldier, he safely predicted, would someday leave the GAR "mustered out by the Angel of Death." As secure as he could feel with that prediction, he surely could not have expected that it would take fifty-six years. And certainly Mr. Shaw would never have dreamed that another man with a Watertown background would fulfill that fate.

Actually, Watertown native Albert Woolson outlived the GAR. He died at the age of 109 in Duluth, Minnesota, in 1956, nailing the coffin for the organization that, three years earlier, had called it quits in Los Angeles.

As for himself, Mr. Shaw came nowhere near challenging the lifespan of his organization. Less than six months after his presentation in Chicago, the fifty-nine-year-old member of the House of Representatives died suddenly in a Washington hotel room, the victim of apoplexy. On February 10, 1901, Mr. Shaw—who had worn the uniform of the Thirty-fifth New York Volunteer Infantry Regiment as witness to seven engagements, including Bull Run, Antietam and Fredericksburg, and who had subsequently served his nation as consul to Toronto and then Manchester, England—answered "the final roll-call."

The fall of the Confederacy and the assassination of President Lincoln were fresh in the nation's conscience when a Union surgeon in Illinois called on his

Monument depicting Albert Woolson, the last surviving Union army veteran, in Ottumwa, Iowa, where he died in 1956. *Courtesy* Watertown Daily Times.

war comrades in 1866 to form a brotherhood. From an organizational meeting in Indianapolis that year evolved an organization that would peak at 409,000 veterans in 1892. Their watchwords: "Fraternity, Charity and Loyalty."

Thirteen posts developed in Jefferson County, the largest of which was opened in Watertown in December 1882, with James A. Dolan, veteran of the Tenth New York Heavy Artillery, as its commander. The post honored the memory of another member of the Tenth, Colonel Joseph Spratt, who died of disease in the waning days of the war. As they had in their fighting days, the veterans adopted a blue uniform coat and slouch hat for their official public appearances.

There were times when the "fraternity" had its rough edges for the Watertown chapter. A clash of personalities in 1913 between Commander Louis C. Greenleaf and Adjutant Angelo D. Pawling became public knowledge after the commander sent a police officer to the Pawling residence to take possession of the post's record book. Mr. Pawling refused to

GAR member Louis Greenleaf. *Courtesy Jefferson County Historical Society.*

surrender the book to the officer, handing it over instead to another member. "I told the officer that the book contained a record of the proceedings of the post for the past several years and that those records were not for the eyes of outsiders," Mr. Pawling said. Mr. Greenleaf did not seek reelection one month later, and in an election in which there were no nominees, Simeon W. Sargent was drafted by the vote of his fellow members.

But that was mild compared to the feud that came in the dust of the Great Depression. John T. Brennan, eighty-one, who had been commander for ten years, canceled the October 1929 meeting, at which elections were to be held, because he was ill. Without his knowledge, however, the meeting was held anyway, and he was unseated by a vote that favored a ninety-one-year-old Methodist minister from Evans Mills, Reverend Alexander F. Beebe.

Mr. Brennan declared the election illegal and asked for an investigation and determination by state GAR officers. A new election was ordered, and Mr. Brennan came out the winner—but not for long. Reverend Beebe appealed the second election, and in February 1930, the judge advocate at the state GAR headquarters ruled that since the Spratt Post senior vice-commander had called the October meeting to order, that election was official. Reverend Beebe became commander. As had happened in October, illness prevented Mr. Brennan from attending the February session. He died thirteen months later.

A death watch prevailed in the 1930s as the north country saw the numbers of its Civil War veterans in inevitable decline. While the Memorial Day parade of 1927 featured fifteen veterans, only two—Reverend Beebe and James M. Waite, eighty-nine-year-old former commander of E.B. Steele Post of Carthage—were on hand five years later.

About 125 people attended a dinner in February 1933 to recognize the recent fiftieth anniversary of the Joe Spratt Post. Eleven members were still alive, but only four were able to attend. Again, Reverend Beebe was holding down the fort, joined by comrades Henry Spencer, eighty-seven; Theodore L. Hunt, eighty-five; and Menzo Yerden, eighty-seven.

GAR member Theodore Hunt. *Courtesy Jefferson County Historical Society.*

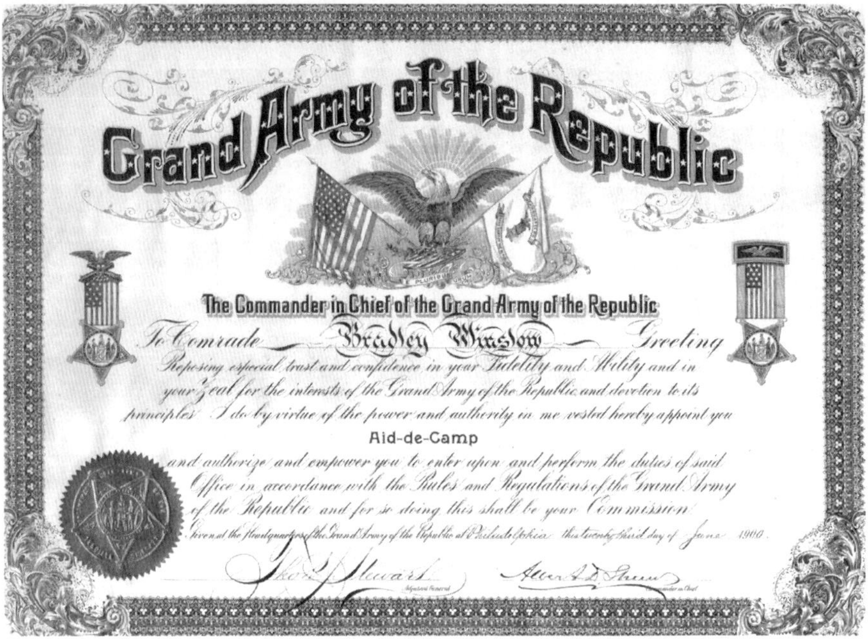

GAR certificate. *Courtesy Jefferson County Historical Society.*

In the spring of 1937, officials estimated that 250 former Union soldiers still lived in New York. There were still four active GAR posts in the north country: Watertown, Dexter, Gouverneur and Massena.

The final countdown began in 1940. On February 4, Lewis County lost its lone survivor, John Salsburg, ninety-two, of Glenfield. Then, one month after the 1941 Memorial Day parade in Watertown had for the first time failed to place Civil War fighters at the head of the march, St. Lawrence County lost its last standard-bearer. William H. Hazelton of Gouverneur died one month shy of his ninety-ninth birthday.

Samuel Graves VanPelt, ninety-eight, Antwerp, was the last holdout for the tri-county area. "An epoch ends," the *Watertown Daily Times* noted in an editorial following his November 23, 1944 death. He was among about 3,500 men from Jefferson County who had taken their place to preserve the Union and put an end to slavery, the paper reported. "In the decades after the Civil War, these men who went away in 1861 and returned in succeeding years played a major part in our development," the editorial continued. "The Joe Spratt Post of the G.A.R. was active for years and once boasted more than 300 members. Now, with the death of Mr. VanPelt, the last survivor passes."

Mr. Woolson became the nation's sole survivor of the Union army in 1953. "I am proud to be the rear guard for such a gallant group of soldiers," he wrote. "I'll try to carry on in the highest tradition of Abe Lincoln's forces till the very end." The end for the old soldier, born on February 11, 1847, in Watertown, came on August 2, 1956.

An "obituary" for the GAR that appeared following Mr. Woolson's death saluted the organization as a "most potent force," one that had fostered the observance of Memorial Day and had "scrutinized school textbooks and scolded publishers who intimated there was virtue in the South." The organization donated funds to benefit crippled and needy veterans and pushed for pensions and government job preference for Union veterans.

Although this somewhat secret society was supposed to be free of politics, it was recognized as a principal instrument in keeping the Republican Party in power.

The passing of Mr. Woolson left three survivors of the Civil War, men who had fought for the Confederacy. The last witness to the war lived to be 116 years old. Walter W. Williams of Franklin, Texas, died in 1959.

Mr. Shaw was also Department of New York GAR commander. Two other veterans from the north country were also honored as state commanders, Major General Newton Martin Curtis of DePeyster in 1888 and Major William H. Daniels of Ogdensburg, who held the post in 1908.

In General Curtis Northern New Yorkers could boast of a Medal of Honor holder. He was recognized for gallantry in leading his troops to victory in the Battle of Fort Fisher, North Carolina, on January 15, 1865. He was wounded four times, losing his left eye. A statue of the eventual congressman was erected in Ogdensburg.

Major Daniels, who during the war was given ten days' leave from the Army of the Potomac so that he could return to Ogdensburg to be married, later had charge of General Sheridan's army train during the Shenandoah Campaign. In civilian life, he was a baker, and he was a Republican Party leader in St. Lawrence County who attended the 1888 national GOP convention.

I have a number of acknowledgements for contributions to this section, with the first going to Jerome Orton of Syracuse, Sons of Union Veterans of the Civil War, who inspired the project. Assisting with research were Watertown city clerk Donna Dutton; Town of Wilna historian Laura M. Prievo; Watertown Times *librarian Esther Daniels;* Times *reporters James R. Donnelly and Steve Virkler; personnel in the surrogate courts of Jefferson, Lewis and St. Lawrence Counties; and Fred H. Rollins and Eileen Bleibtrey of the Jefferson County Historical Society. The book* Whispers From the Past, *by Harold I. Sanderson of Alexandria Bay, was used for reference.*

THE LAST NINETY SURVIVORS

The following list is based on research into names that appeared at various times in *Watertown Daily Times* news stories. The names are compiled in order of the veterans' dates of death. I regret any oversights that might have resulted in the omission of some Civil War veterans who died after 1903.

1903—James A. Dolan, Watertown. Pension attorney. Served with Tenth New York Heavy Artillery. Charter commander of Joe Spratt Post, Grand Army of the Republic, Watertown.

January 7, 1910—Major General Newton Martin Curtis, seventy-four, DePeyster. Postmaster, assemblyman and congressman. Served with Sixteenth New York Infantry at Battle of Fort Fisher, wounded, received Medal of Honor for gallantry. Commander of GAR, Department of New York.

October 25, 1914—General Bradley Winslow, eighty-three, Watertown. Jefferson County district attorney and Watertown mayor. Served with 35th Regiment, New York Volunteer Infantry, at Rappahannock Station, Groveton and Bull Run; with 186th Regiment, New York Volunteer Infantry, at Petersburg and Fort Mahone, wounded. Honored by President Lincoln with rank of brevet brigadier general for "gallant and meritorious conduct in the assault before Petersburg." Charter member and first vice-commander of New York Department, GAR, aide-de-camp of National Commander Albert D. Shaw and commander of Joe Pratt Post, Watertown.

January 1915—Luther N. Stevens, Chaumont. Served with Tenth New York Heavy Artillery.

December 24, 1915—Lewis Roberts, eighty-six, Watertown. Machinist. Served with Seventh Battery, Wisconsin Light Artillery, at Chancellorsville and Corinth, wounded.

December 24, 1915—John Calvin Relyea, Pamelia. Served with Tenth New York Heavy Artillery.

February 1, 1916—William H. Daniels, seventy-seven, Ogdensburg. Baker and politician. Served with Sixteenth New York Volunteers and later with the Army of the Potomac in the Shenandoah Campaign. Department of New York commander, GAR, and Ogdensburg post commander.

November 20, 1916—John F. Lambie, Northampton, Massachusetts, previously of Watertown.

December 26, 1916—General Edwin A. Merritt, eighty-eight, Potsdam. Pierrepont town supervisor, state assemblyman, New York Port collector and consul general to London. Served with Sixtieth New York Volunteers in several battles, including Lookout Mountain.

January 27, 1917—Joseph H. Pearsall, seventy-five, Watertown. New York Air Brake Company pattern and drafting department and instructor of mathematics and engineering at YMCA. Served with 114th New York Volunteers and with Engineering Corps in Shenandoah Valley, surveying for mapping. Member of Joe Spratt Post, GAR, Watertown.

The Last Eighty

January 27, 1917—Martin Leach, seventy-nine, Carthage. Tanner. Served with 186th Infantry and 10th New York Heavy Artillery.

January 2, 1918—Mark Anthony Wiley, seventy-nine, Watertown. Farmer. Served with Thirty-fifth New York Volunteer Infantry. Member of Joe Spratt Post, GAR, Watertown.

November 25, 1918—Joseph E. Howland, town of Rutland. Served with Tenth New York Heavy Artillery.

February 25, 1919—Charles M. Beard, eighty-four, Watertown. Building caretaker. Served with 186th New York Infantry at Hatcher's Run and Petersburg. Member of Joe Spratt Post, GAR, Watertown.

February 11, 1920—Simeon W. Sargent, seventy-eight, Watertown. Farmer. Served with Tenth New York Heavy Artillery. Commander of Joe Spratt Post, GAR, Watertown.

February 26, 1920—Major Louis C. Greenleaf, seventy-nine, Watertown. Banker, partner in Sloat & Greenleaf Lumber Company, first Watertown city treasurer, county treasurer and city councilman. Served with Thirty-fifth New York Volunteers Regiment at the Rappahannock River, Fainesville, Groveton, Bull Run, Fairfax Court House, South Mountain, Antietam and Fredericksburg, wounded in two battles. Commander of Joe Spratt Post, GAR, Watertown.

September 13, 1920—Daniel McIntyre, seventy-six, Watertown. City public works department. Served with Tenth New York Artillery at Petersburg. Member of Joe Spratt Post, GAR, Watertown.

February 22, 1923—Alexander R. Wilson, seventy-seven, Watertown. Picture framer. Served with 102nd Pennsylvania Volunteer Infantry. Member of Joe Spratt Post, GAR, Watertown.

May 2, 1924—Orville J. Van Wormer, eighty, Watertown. Police officer and real estate agent. Served with 186th New York Volunteers at Petersburg. Told of when he talked with President Lincoln. Commander of Joe Spratt Post, GAR, Watertown.

August 28, 1924—Charles Watson Sloat, eighty-three, Watertown. Partner in Sloat & Greenleaf lumber company, later Sloat & Son. Served with Ninety-fourth New York Volunteer Infantry at Cedar Mountain, Bull Run, South Mountain, Antietam, Fredericksburg, Chancellorsville, Mine Run, Cold Harbor, Petersburg and Gettysburg, where he was taken prisoner.

The Last Seventy

June 25, 1925—Demertis L. Cornwell, seventy-six, Watertown. Grocer and county food administrator during World War I. Served with 186th New York Infantry at Petersburg. Commander of Joe Spratt Post, GAR, Watertown.

October 23, 1926—Lyle B. Bence, ninety, Carthage. Teacher, store clerk and later a traveling representative for a cigar company. Served with 186th Regiment at Petersburg. Member of E.B. Steele Post, GAR, Carthage.

March 22, 1927—George S. Parsons, eighty-three, Gouverneur. Served with Eleventh New York Cavalry at Washington. Member of Joe Spratt Post, GAR, Watertown.

July 7, 1927—Eugene G. Clark, eighty-three, Watertown. Restaurateur and baggage man. Served with Tenth New York Heavy Artillery in Battle of the Wilderness, Petersburg and Richmond, wounded. Commander of Joe Spratt Post, GAR, Watertown.

GAR member Demertis Cornwell. *Courtesy Jefferson County Historical Society.*

August 2, 1927—Joseph Field, eighty-three, Watertown. Carpenter. Served with Ninety-fourth New York Regiment at Cedar Mountain,

Shiloh and Bull Run, wounded. Member of Joe Spratt Post, GAR, Watertown.

October 8, 1927—Robert Tennant, eighty-one, Smithville. School janitor. Served with 106th New York Volunteers in several battles, including Gettysburg. Member of Joe Spratt Post, GAR, Watertown.

November 5, 1927—Newton D. Chase, eighty-one, Rochester, previously of Watertown. Railroad and milk delivery. Served with 186th New York Infantry Volunteers at Petersburg. Member of Joe Spratt Post, GAR, Watertown.

January 15, 1928—Angelo D. Pawling, eighty-two, Watertown. President, W.H. Cook Medicine Company. Served with Tenth New York Heavy Artillery at Battle of the Wilderness. Charter member of Joe Spratt Post, GAR, Watertown.

February 4, 1928—John Varley, eighty-five, Carthage. Policeman and Town of Wilna overseer of the poor. Served with Tenth New York Heavy Artillery in the Battle of the Wilderness and in Shenandoah Valley.

March 30, 1928—Clytus Shepard, eighty-six, Winter Haven, Florida, previously of Watertown. Farmer. War service unspecified. Member of Joe Spratt Post, GAR, Watertown.

THE LAST SIXTY

July 19, 1928—Norman S. Snell, ninety, Watertown. Shoe store clerk, employee of Hitchcock Lamp Company, restaurateur and noted astronomer. Served with Fourteenth New York Artillery in several campaigns. Member of Joe Spratt Post, GAR, Watertown.

November 20, 1928—William Shinners, eighty, Watertown. Trainer of racehorses. Served with 186th New York Volunteer Infantry at Petersburg. Member of Joe Spratt Post, GAR, Watertown.

January 8, 1929—Marcus Reed, served with 186th New York Volunteer Infantry.

March 31, 1929—William O'Horo, eighty, Carthage. Pension attorney. Served with Forty-fourth New York Infantry. Member of E.B. Steele Post, GAR, Carthage.

April 13, 1929—George Christman, eighty-four, West Carthage. Well driller, quarrying. Served with Thirty-fifth Infantry, New York Volunteers, and with Fourteenth Regiment, New York Volunteer Heavy Artillery, at Falmouth, Richmond, Cedar Mountain, Bull Run, Antietam, Fredericksburg, Chancellorsville, the Wilderness, Cold Harbor and Petersburg, wounded. Member of E.B. Steele Post, GAR, Carthage.

June 25, 1929—Gilbert Chapman, Cape Vincent. Served with Tenth New York Heavy Artillery.

August 18, 1929—Theodore Henry, eighty-one, Watertown. Farmer and mason. Member of Joe Spratt Post, GAR, Watertown.

September 28, 1929—Patrick Finley, eighty-two, Carthage. Farmer.

October 16, 1929—William M. Rice, eighty-two, Watertown. Spinner at Dexter Woolen Mill and carpenter. Served with Tenth New York Heavy Artillery.

November 5, 1929—Henry A. Drappo, eighty-one, Watertown, previously of Harrisville. Surveyor and forester. Served with 186th New York Infantry. Member of Joe Spratt Post, GAR, Watertown.

GAR member William M. Rice. *Courtesy Jefferson County Historical Society.*

THE LAST FIFTY

November 17, 1929—Fernando Lansing Rockwood, eighty-two, West Carthage. Police officer and Town of Champion justice of the peace. Served with Twentieth New York Cavalry at Harpers Ferry, Norfolk and Richmond. Member of E.B. Steele Post, GAR, Carthage.

November 30, 1929—Greenleaf H. Farr, eighty-three, Pamelia, previously of Ellisburg and Cape Vincent. Farmer. Served with Fourteenth New York Heavy Artillery. Member of Joe Spratt Post, GAR, Watertown.

January 1, 1930—John Goodenough, eighty-three, Theresa, previously of New Bremen and Carthage. Woodworker. Served with Fifth New York Heavy Artillery at Washington and Harpers Ferry. Rendered deaf by cannon blast. Member of GAR.

January 7, 1930—Jehu F. Osborn, eighty-two, Carthage. Served with 186th Regiment, New York Volunteers, in siege of Petersburg and Battle of Appomattox. Member of E.B. Steele Post, GAR, Carthage.

May 3, 1930—Nelson B. Felshaw, eighty-eight, West Carthage, previously of Constableville. Jeweler. Served with Fifth New York Heavy Artillery.

July 28, 1930—Richard Fluno, ninety, Dexter, previously of Natural Bridge. Farmer. Served with Fourteenth New York Heavy Artillery, taken prisoner. Member of Joe Spratt Post, GAR, Watertown.

August 29, 1930—Charles Beerman, Gouverneur.

October 14, 1930—Charles P. Walker, eighty-eight, Carthage, previously of Martinsburg. Served with Fourteenth New York Heavy Artillery, wounded twice. Commander of E.B. Steele Post, GAR, Carthage.

January 8, 1931—Lawson Tripp, eighty-nine, Watertown. Tanner. Served with Ninety-fourth Regiment, New York Volunteer Infantry, at Cedar Mountain, Bull Run, Antietam, Chancellorsville, Gettysburg, Potomac, Cold Harbor and Petersburg. Taken prisoner at Gettysburg. Member of Joe Spratt Post, GAR, Watertown.

March 30, 1931—John T. Brennan, eighty-two, Watertown. Riverboat captain and with finishing department at International Paper, Glen Park. Served with Tenth New York Heavy Artillery at Cold Harbor, Petersburg, Cedar Creek and Richmond. Commander of Joe Spratt Post, GAR, Watertown.

April 6, 1931—John E. Bogardus, eighty-five, Brasie Corners. Farmer. Served in the Fourteenth New York Heavy Artillery at Petersburg and with the First Rhode Island Light Artillery in the Shenandoah Valley. Member of Erwin Barnes Post, GAR, Gouverneur.

June 29, 1931—Samuel Dawson, eighty-five, Watertown. Railroad laborer and New York Air Brake Company employee. Served with Sixteenth New York Heavy Artillery at Petersburg, Richmond and Battle of West Point, wounded. Member and "officer of the day" of Joe Spratt Post, GAR, Watertown.

June 26, 1931—Edwin B. Humphreys, eighty-eight, Gouverneur. Ironworker. Served with Twenty-second Regiment, New York Cavalry. Commander of GAR post in New York City and member of E.H. Barnes Post, Gouverneur.

July 3, 1931—Silas Wright Payne, eighty-three, Gouverneur. Owner of Payne Drug Company. Served with Twentieth Regiment, New York Cavalry, under General Cushing at Fort Monroe. Commander of Erwin Barnes Post, GAR, 1930.

July 12, 1931—Charles B. Van Namee, eighty-six, Gouverneur. Farmer. Served with 152nd Regiment, New York Infantry, in several campaigns.

October 16, 1931—Dr. George D. Hewitt, ninety-four, West Carthage. Physician, West Carthage village president and Town of Champion supervisor. Served with 186th New York Volunteer Infantry at Hancock Station, Stony Creek and other battles, as assistant sergeant in medical department. Member of GAR.

April 28, 1932—Charles D. Bingham, eighty-six, Watertown. Bookkeeper, executive with Watertown manufacturing companies and mayor of Watertown. Served with Third New York Light Artillery at Petersburg, Richmond. Commander of Joe Spratt Post, GAR, Watertown, at time of death.

GAR member Charles Bingham. *Courtesy Jefferson County Historical Society.*

May 1, 1932—Robert H. Sheley, ninety, Omar. Boat livery operator. Served with Tenth New York Heavy Artillery at Petersburg.

May 18, 1932—Frederick A. Crandall, eighty-seven, Watertown. Printer. Served with Ninety-second New York Infantry. Member of Joe Spratt Post, GAR, Watertown.

May 22, 1932—Horace W. Freeman, eighty-eight, Adams Center. Farmer. Served with First New York Light Artillery in forty battles, including South Mountain, Antietam, Balls Bluff, Fredericksburg, Gettysburg, Chancellorsville, Cold Harbor and Bull Run. Rendered deaf by cannon blast.

December 12, 1932—Edward B. Moore, eighty-nine, Point Peninsula (died at Grand Rapids, Michigan). Farmer. Served with Tenth New York Heavy Artillery at Cold Harbor and siege of Petersburg. Member of Joe Spratt Post, GAR, Watertown.

January 3, 1933—Charles H. Sprague, ninety-one, Denver, Colorado, previously of Henderson and Watertown. Clothing merchant and real estate agent. Served with Tenth New York Heavy Artillery at Appomattox. Member of Joe Spratt Post, GAR, Watertown.

July 20, 1933—William Hart, eighty-eight, East Hounsfield. Farmer and meat marketer. Served at Richmond, Hatches Run, Poplar Grove Church and Five Forks, wounded. Member of Joe Spratt Post, GAR, Watertown.

January 24, 1934—J. Mills Corwin, eighty-nine, West Carthage, previously of Harrisville. Tanner. Served with 132nd Pennsylvania Regiment and later with the 52nd Pennsylvania Regiment at Antietam and Fredericksburg. Commander of E.B. Steele Post, GAR, Carthage.

March 10, 1934—Elijah Cobb, 100, town of Hounsfield. Farmer and town road commissioner. Served with 186th New York Volunteers at Nottoway, Fort Mahone and Petersburg. Member of Joseph K. Barnes Post, GAR, Sackets Harbor, and later of Joe Spratt Post, Watertown.

The Last Twenty-Five

March 15, 1934—George W. Wood, ninety-three, West Carthage. Farmer. Served with First New York Light Artillery and Twentieth New York Cavalry.

January 9, 1935—James O. Ault, eighty-six, Adams. Mail carrier. Served with New York Volunteer Cavalry at Petersburg and Five Forks. Member of DeAlton Cooper Post, GAR, Adams.

December 25, 1935—Theodore Lansing Hunt, eighty-eight, Watertown. Carpenter and superintendent of school buildings in Watertown. Served with Eleventh New York Regular Infantry, witnessed the siege at Richmond while lying seriously ill near battlefield. Junior commander of Joe Spratt Post, GAR, Watertown.

February 6, 1936—Armand Hubbard, ninety, Carthage. Operated livery stable and Hatch House hotel. Served with 186th New York Volunteer Infantry.

July 10, 1936—Reverend Almon J. Foster, ninety-two, Watertown. Pentecostal minister. Served with Forty-seventh New York Infantry in the battles of Seven Pines and Fishers Landing, wounded. Member of Joe Spratt Post, GAR, Watertown.

August 24, 1936—Philo Radley, ninety-two, Lowville. Farmer. Served with Fifth New York Heavy Artillery.

September 6, 1936—Hezekiah Bowen, Gouverneur.

October 30, 1936—Jefferson D. Shultz, ninety-two, Lyons Falls. Railroad surveyor and construction engineer. Served with Fifth New York Artillery in several battles, including Shenandoah Valley. Member of GAR post in Elmira.

January 16, 1937—Charles A. Bennett, ninety, Lowville, previously of the town of Harrisburg. Farmer. Served with Fifth New York Heavy Artillery at Harpers Ferry, Cedar Creek and Maryland Heights. Boasted of shaking hands with President Lincoln.

March 21, 1937—Reverend Alexander F. Beebe, ninety-seven, Pamelia, previously of Evans Mills. Methodist minister. Served with Nineteenth New York Regiment and Third New York Light Infantry in many battles, including Petersburg and Richmond. Boasted of speaking and shaking hands with President Lincoln. Commander of Joe Spratt Post, GAR, Watertown.

April 27, 1937—Alvin L. Barber, ninety-second, DeKalb Junction. Railroad worker. Served with Sixtieth New York Volunteers at Bull Run, Antietam, Chancellorsville, Gettysburg, Chattanooga, Lookout Mountain, Tree Creek, Dallas, Kenesaw Mountain and Atlanta. Member of E.H. Barnes Post, GAR, Gouverneur.

April 29, 1937—Reverend Albert M. Ash, ninety-five, Dexter. Methodist Episcopal minister. Served with Fifth New York Light Artillery at Washington, D.C., and Maryland Heights. Member of Julius Broadbent Post, GAR, Dexter.

November 8, 1937—Henry H. Rogers, ninety-six, Gouverneur. Carpenter. Served with Sixteenth New York Infantry in at least twenty battles, including Antietam, Bull Run, South Mountain, Fredericksburg and Salem Heights, where he was wounded. Member of E.H. Barnes Post, GAR, Gouverneur.

December 24, 1937—Menzo Yerden, ninety-two, Black River. Farmer. Served with 110th New York Volunteer Infantry in Louisiana. Member of Joe Spratt Post, GAR, Watertown.

June 23, 1938—Clark Taft Van Valkenburg, ninety-one, Lowville. Steam mill operator and farmer. Served with Eighty-first New York Infantry at Cold Harbor, Petersburg and Bull Run.

February 15, 1939—Reverend Reuben Kline, ninety-four, Port Leyden. Methodist Episcopal minister. Served with Twenty-first Regiment, New York Cavalry, had horse shot from under him in battle. Guilford D. Bailey Post, GAR, Glenfield.

June 17, 1939—Jacob A. Barlett, ninety-two, West Carthage. Trucker, bus driver and cabbie. Served with 186th New York Infantry at Petersburg, wounded.

August 11, 1939—Benjamin M. Miller, ninety-four, Gouverneur. Carpenter. Served with Twentieth New York Cavalry in several conflicts. Charter member of E.H. Barnes Post, GAR, Gouverneur.

February 4, 1940—John Salsburg, ninety-two, Glenfield. Woodsman, contractor and guide. Served with Fifth New York Infantry at Petersburg and Richmond. Charter member and last survivor of Gilford D. Bailey Post, GAR, Glenfield.

June 28, 1941—William H. Hazelton, ninety-eight, Gouverneur. Miner, farmer, logger, cemetery superintendent and tax collector. Served with 142nd New York Volunteer Infantry in thirty battles, from Kiawah Island to Fort Fisher. Commander of E.H. Barnes Post, GAR, Gouverneur.

GAR member Henry Spencer. *Courtesy Jefferson County Historical Society.*

November 1, 1941—Henry Spencer, ninety-five, Watertown. Farmer. Served with Thirteenth New York Gun Boat Regiment at Portsmouth and Norfolk, Virginia, and along James River. Senior vice-commander of Joe Spratt Post, GAR, Watertown.

February 26, 1942—James Merritt Waite, ninety-eight, Brownville, previously of West Carthage. Served with Fourteenth New York Heavy Artillery at Spotsylvania, Cold Harbor, the Wilderness Campaign and the battle of Wendon Railroad, Richmond, wounded. Commander of Joe Spratt Post, GAR, Watertown, and member of E.B. Steele Post, GAR, Carthage.

May 17, 1942—John Hunter, 107, town of Orleans, previously of Henderson. Great Lakes sailor. Served with Union navy in Battle of

Mobile Bay, at Vicksburg and in other water battles. Member of Piper Post, GAR, Henderson.

November 23, 1944—Samuel Graves VanPelt, ninety-eight, Antwerp. Construction worker, woodworker and farmer. Served with Twentieth Division, New York Cavalry at Norfolk. Member of E.B. Steele Post, GAR, Carthage, and later Joe Spratt Post, Watertown.

August 2, 1956—Albert Woolson, 109, Duluth, Minnesota, previously of Watertown. Wood-turner and machinist. Served with First Minnesota Heavy Artillery at Gettysburg and in Tennessee. Senior vice–commander in chief, national GAR.

References were found to the following names, but no subsequent information was found: Lewis J. Baron of Constableville, John H. Carpenter of Evans Mills, Duane Chapman of Smithville, J. Coons of Carthage, Norman George of Theresa, Ransom Green of Theresa, William McIntyre of Gouverneur, David MacIntosh of Harrisville, Peter Rederick of Gouverneur, DeAlton Cooper of Watertown, S.D. Demare of Watertown and Fred H. Gould of Watertown.

Old Soldiers Fade Away

Two Union Veterans Lived Well into the Twentieth Century

John Hunter said that he was ready to die.

One of the last two Civil War veterans residing in Jefferson County was observing his 102nd birthday in July 1936 at his Roberts Corners home in the town of Henderson, New York.

"When a man gets to be my age, life becomes a burden to him," he told a *Watertown Daily Times* reporter. "This will be my last birthday. I don't expect to go anywhere this summer because my heart is getting weaker." He fooled himself. Come Election Day in November 1940, at age 106, he was keeping alive his perfect record of casting a ballot in presidential elections, dating back to the 1856 campaign, when Democrat James Buchanan was elected.

The staunch Republican proudly disclosed his vote for Wendell Willkie, and again he made a prediction. This, he said, would probably be the last time he would vote in a presidential election. It was a pretty safe prediction, since he'd have to live to be 110. And this time, he was right. On May 17, 1942, about nineteen months after he saw his candidate go down in defeat, he surrendered the distinction of being New York's oldest Civil War veteran. He was 107. In Antwerp, meanwhile, the county still had a survivor of the War Between the States, 95-year-old Samuel G. VanPelt. He would live to see three more birthdays.

It was 150 years ago, on April 12 and 13, 1861, when an assault on Fort Sumter, near Charleston, South Carolina, triggered the war fought to preserve the Union. A year later, John Hunter signed up, bringing his sailing

John Hunter (dark suit) at 105. *Courtesy* Watertown Daily Times.

experience to Abraham Lincoln's navy. In the second year of the conflict, a teenager from Carthage, Sam VanPelt, left home to join the cavalry. Hunter would see battle against an ironclad, and VanPelt would be at Appomattox, Virginia, when General Robert E. Lee surrendered.

John Hunter had a few warriors in his family background when he was born on July 14, 1834. His father, Elijah, had served under Major General James Wilkinson in the United States' unsuccessful campaign along the St. Lawrence River during the War of 1812. His maternal grandfather was a colonel under General George Washington's command during the Revolutionary War.

Despite their American roots, Elijah and Easter Youngs Hunter moved to Canada, where John was born in Violet, Ontario. He was just a young boy when his mother died, and at age seven, he was bound out by his father to serve on a lumber vessel.

Crusty seamen likely called him "horse boy," since that was his first job on a timber schooner operated between Bay of Quinte and Oswego. He rode a horse that hauled a device to direct a line of hewed timber being either loaded or offloaded. After he had a year or so under his belt, he became a "sailor boy" aboard lake vessels. His immediate future was set, with his next several years committed to sailing the Great Lakes and becoming familiar with all the ports from Sackets Harbor to Duluth, Minnesota.

Testing different waters, Hunter eventually became second officer aboard a supply ship that sailed between Philadelphia, Pennsylvania, and New Orleans. That was his role when the Union and the Confederacy began exchanging gunfire. At New Orleans in 1862, the twenty-eight-year-old sailor enlisted in the Union navy. "My entire stay in southern waters was spent on Navy boats chasing blockade runners," he said in one of several interviews.

In a fleet commanded by Admiral David G. Farragut, he was assigned to a wooden screw sloop of war, the USS *Monongahela*, and was aboard for the naval battle of Mobile Bay, Alabama, on August 5, 1864. "I was one of the sailors that poured shot into the hull of the *Tennessee* [a Confederate ironclad, twin of the *Merrimac*]," he told a reporter. With its sloping roof-shaped deck of railroad iron, the craft readily repelled forty-pound shots.

He said that the *Monongahela*, equipped with a long steel prow for ramming, rushed the *Tennessee*. As the gunboat sheered past, Mr. Hunter was one of the gunners who poured a broadside of shot into the side of the craft where timbers below the railroad iron had become exposed.

A moment later, a monitor (a small Federal warship) shot away wheel chains at the rudder head, and the *Tennessee* lay helpless, with smoke pouring from its hatches. He recalled how the crew of the captured ship scrambled out and deserted it, and the *Tennessee* became a prize of the *Monongahela*.

Hunter's boat was also sent to help break through defenses at Vicksburg. The *Monongahela*, which was a steamer converted to a gunboat, was hit by a Confederate shot through the paddle wheel and was compelled to turn back and retire from battle. "I was aboard the *Monongahela* when our rudder was destroyed," Hunter wrote. "We drifted out of the range of the fighting and repaired her. After we returned to the rest of the squadron, we succeeded in getting by the enemy forts, and we opened the bay."

After the victory, he was transferred to the West Gulf squadron. "This group of ships was stationed in the vicinity of Galveston, Texas," Hunter said. "It was during this time that the Spanish brig, the *Echo*, was captured. This was a sleek vessel used in running cotton out of the ports on the Gulf of Mexico. The cotton was destined for Europe." He said he participated in the capture of a number of cotton boats.

With three years of war behind him, he was discharged on August 11, 1865, at Philadelphia. He traveled to Henderson, married Mary Jane Peters in 1866 and went back to his old life, spending the next eighteen years as a Great Lakes seaman.

As he entered the second half-century of his life, he became a landlubber, settling in 1883 on a small farm at Roberts Corners, where he built a home.

Mary Jane Hunter died in 1901, and the old sailor soon married Susan Kellar David of Adams Center. She lived to be ninety-five, dying in 1929.

The dutiful John Hunter birthday watch by local newspapers appears to have started shortly before he hit the century mark. In the dead of winter of 1934, his 100th celebration six months away, a *Watertown Daily Times* story reported that the war veteran walked a few miles and then, upon returning home, offered to chop some wood. No way, said his son, John.

"I can saw wood just as well as you can," he protested to his 55-year-old son. At 103, he was still pulling mustard plants from a corn patch on his farm. In an interview before his 104th birthday, he offered his view about world events of the day. The nation was "paralyzed by capital," he said, explaining that "we have too many grab-alls who have all the money and can tell the rest of the people what to do."

Despite that impression, he felt that labor unions were "riding too high" and that employers "should have the right to kick out a man if he can't do the work without all the rest of the workers going on strike."

And war was brewing in Europe. "Trouble with airplanes is that they fly over cities and drop bombs and kill a lot of women and children, like they're doing in Spain. I think planes ought to be outlawed."

Just a few weeks after his 105th birthday, his eyesight having deserted him, Mr. Hunter was participating in a historical event, the July 1939 dedication of the Thousand Islands bridges. A Toronto radio station interviewed him atop the Canadian span.

Then came that 1940 election, when the Republican lost his vote with Willkie. If he always voted by his party line, he helped send Lincoln, Grant, Hayes, Garfield, Harrison, McKinley, Teddy Roosevelt, Taft, Harding, Coolidge and Hoover to the White House. He witnessed the election of four Democrats: Buchanan, Cleveland, Wilson and Franklin Roosevelt.

Veterans of the blue and gray uniforms were invited to attend the seventy-fifth anniversary observance of the Battle of Gettysburg in July 1938, and

John Hunter received his invitation. He didn't go. "I'd like to have gone first rate, but I can't stand long trips in the auto," he explained.

But the gentleman from Antwerp, Samuel Graves VanPelt, who was approaching his ninety-second birthday, made the trip. Escorted on the all-expenses-paid journey by his grandnephew from Watertown, L. Wadsworth VanPelt, he didn't get to see the main speaker, President Franklin D. Roosevelt. "We felt it was too much of a job in the hot weather to get through the crowd," Samuel told the *Times* upon his return. But he mentioned having made a friendly acquaintance with a former Confederate cavalry captain, Robert E. Miles, ninety-eight.

Wadsworth VanPelt told a reporter that he was impressed "by the spirit of courage and determination shown by those veterans, some of them in wheelchairs and hardly able to move. It was a great lesson for any of the younger people who were there to learn." Samuel VanPelt didn't serve at Gettysburg. Actually, he didn't become a soldier until about a month after the battle.

Mr. VanPelt was apparently one of those old soldiers who didn't care to discuss his war experiences. What is known is that he was seventeen, working at a butter tub factory in Carthage, when he enlisted in the Union army on August 6, 1863. He was assigned to Company E, Twentieth New York Volunteer Cavalry Regiment, and served for nearly two years. The regiment was with defense forces in the Army of the James River and, later, with the Tenth Army Corps, seeing action in several battles in Virginia.

After the war, Mr. VanPelt was involved in the construction of the Utica and Black River Railway and later worked at the M.P. Mason woodworking shop in Carthage. He eventually took up farming near Copenhagen, where his wife of thirty-one years, Ruth Fogg VanPelt, died in May 1905.

VanPelt married Martha E. Payne of Copenhagen in December 1906, and after completing his twenty-three years of farming, the couple moved to Antwerp. Mrs. VanPelt was among survivors when he died at age ninety-eight in November 1944.

The last surviving Union soldier was also a Jefferson County man, although he was living in Duluth, Minnesota. Albert Woolson was 109 when he died on August 2, 1956.

Three Confederates died after Mr. Woolson, the last of whom, Walter W. Williams, was 116 when he died in 1959 in Franklin, Texas.

Albert Woolson, Jefferson County native, was the last surviving Union soldier. He was 109 when he died in 1956. *Courtesy* Watertown Daily Times.

Mr. Miles, Mr. VanPelt's acquaintance at Gettysburg, lived to be 102. His war experience included the Battle of Antietam.

The book Whispers From the Past, *written by Harold I. Sanderson, was a reference for this section. Robert Hutchinson of Rodman drew our attention to John Hunter. Lisa Carr,* Times *librarian, assisted with research.*

A Civil War Hero Missed His Chance to Change History

Where was "Grampa Jack" of Smithville when President Lincoln needed him most? After all, only seventeen months earlier, the one-armed soldier, by his own account, had shielded the president from would-be assassins. But on that fateful evening of April 14, 1865, Ford's Theatre in Washington was out of sight and out of mind for the newlywed officer.

Grampa Jack, as some of his descendants in southern Jefferson County call him, was Major Frederick R. Jackson, veteran of the Seventh Connecticut Volunteers in the Union army and winner of the prestigious Medal of Honor. He lived in Smithville, but not until many years after he was wounded on a Civil War battlefield and many years after he walked and chatted with the sixteenth president of the United States.

So who was this Major Jackson? He is prominent enough to have had a bridge named for him in 1991 in North Haven, Connecticut. He was born there on February 18, 1844, a son of Benjamin Hall and Harriet Bradley Jackson. He must have been an intelligent young man because at the age of seventeen, he was all set to enter Yale. And permit me a bit of pride here if I boast that he was also a newspaper reporter. That is what Walter Gawrych, first selectman of North Haven in 1989, wrote for the *Quadtown Advisor*, a community newspaper.

When the conflict over states' rights came along, the young Mr. Jackson was determined to join the fight to preserve the Union. He came from fighting and patriotic stock, his obituary reveals. In 1638, his ancestors came

After losing his left arm in battle, Civil War soldier Frederick R. Jackson was held as a prisoner of war. *Courtesy of Joyce Crumb, Adams, New York.*

to the New World and became members of the New Haven, Connecticut settlement. In the next century, when the colonies fought to break away from British rule, among the volunteers in the freedom fight were two men who would someday be his grandfathers.

Mr. Jackson enlisted in July 1861. A life-altering incident took place on June 16, 1862, when he was an eighteen-year-old first sergeant. He was at James Island in South Carolina. The brief explanation for his Medal of Honor describes what happened: "Having his left arm shot away in a charge on the enemy, he continued on duty, taking part in a second and a third charge until he fell exhausted from the loss of blood."

His obituary, which appeared on February 18, 1925, in the *Watertown Daily Times*, gave an expanded account:

> *He was struck on the elbow…and his arm was severely shattered. With his other hand he seized the splintered arm and pressed it tightly to his side to prevent as far as possible the flow of blood. He plunged again into the battle and his regiment, after repeated charges, retired. When the troops*

> *were finally repulsed,* [he] *fell from loss of blood and lay on the battlefield amid intense firing for 17 hours before he finally was taken prisoner by the rebel forces and removed to a hospital.*

He was taken to meet the surgeon's knife, the story continued: "He was one of 14 soldiers taken to the amputating room of the hospital, and there his arm was amputated without the use of chloroform."

The soldier was kept prisoner until October 12, 1862, according to records at the National Archives in Washington. A week later, as he was being discharged from the army, he met the president, who had been informed by other soldiers of Mr. Jackson's heroics and his injury. In a letter written by Mr. Jackson nearly three decades later, he quoted the president. "I want to give this brave boy a Medal of Honor, and I wish you would personally see that he has one," Mr. Lincoln said to Secretary of War Edwin M. Stanton. Then, dismissing the soldier, Mr. Lincoln promised him a commission.

Mr. Jackson returned to Connecticut, much to the surprise of his mother, who had received word from the Department of War that he had been killed in action. The wounded warrior was nineteen when he received, in the fall of 1863, the commission the president had promised, along with Mr. Lincoln's invitation to Washington. He went to the War Department, and there he had an unexpected meeting with the president. "He recognized me and stopped and talked with me. In a few moments he said abruptly, 'By the way, you have got your Medal of Honor all right, I suppose?'" But he had not. "Then he asked me to go with him and took me straight to Secretary Stanton's room and said 'Our little lieutenant says he hasn't received his Medal of Honor yet. Did you send it to him?'" Mr. Stanton confirmed that he had not and fulfilled the command two weeks later.

Now we approach the time where documented history and the soldier's accounts fail to agree. What is correctly recorded is that Mr. Lincoln selected the one-armed soldier to command his honor guard for his trip to Gettysburg for the November 19, 1863 dedication of the national cemetery there. But Lincoln historians both in Gettysburg and in Illinois, "the Land of Lincoln," say that they are unaware of the Jackson version of what happened while the president and his guard detail were en route to the famed delivery of the Gettysburg Address. It was November 18, 1863, the day before Abraham Lincoln would pull a piece of paper from his pocket and read, "Four score and seven years ago…"

I refer now to a story from an unidentified newspaper, which quoted Mr. Jackson extensively:

> *It was well that the great war president had a guard on that occasion, for an attempt was made in Baltimore by a gang of roughs to get into his car. I had 50 men on the train as a guard. We arrived in Baltimore early in the morning, and as the cars were being slowly hauled by horses through the city, the crowd jumped upon the platform of the private car in which sat Lincoln and Stanton. It was a silent crowd that received us as the train rolled into the depot, just such a crowd as would be bent on making trouble.*
>
> *We tried to get the fellows off the platform, but they persisted and packed on like sardines. I at last ordered my men to use the bayonet and we pricked several of them before they would jump down.*
>
> *Secretary Stanton always claimed that those fellows were bent on assassinating the president and that only my guard saved him.*

The *Baltimore Sun* checked its archives for me and found a story about the president passing through that day, but it did not find anything describing the skirmish on the train. A story in the *Sun* listed Lieutenant F.R. Jackson in command of the First Invalid Regiment honor guard on the train.

"There was quite a crowd of persons at the Camden Station upon the arrival of the train, and the President was repeatedly cheered," the story noted. Mr. Lincoln "came to the platform of the car in which he was several times and acknowledged the cheering, and at the same time gave every one a chance to have a good look at him." The story did disclose, however, that "much sport and a great amount of crowding was indulged in to obtain a sight of the distinguished passengers."

There could have been more to the "crowding" than what was reported, according to John Heiser, historian at the Gettysburg National Military Park. "If there were any attempts such as described [by Mr. Jackson], they were not written about in newspapers of the day and the reporting of any events such as this may have been suppressed by the Pinkerton agents," Mr. Heiser said.

A letter written by Major Jackson in 1894, reprinted in the book *The Badge of Gallantry*, by Lieutenant Colonel Joseph B. Mitchell, addressed a different war topic, but it may offer some answers to any questions about his veracity. "I never sought fame, honor or notoriety," he said. "I don't care to tell of my own deeds. I always dreaded to. It seemed so egotistical."

More service lay ahead for the one-armed officer. He was put in charge of Fort Kearney, one of the Northern defenses for the divided nation's capital. Here he stood his ground for five days and five hours, his two companies countering the July 1864 attack of Confederate general Jubal A. Early. It could have been a blood bath if General Early had known how superior his numbers were to those of the Union defenders. But Early fought conservatively and then had to pull back when Union reinforcements arrived.

During that waning period of the war, Jackson developed a fellowship with the president, as related in the unidentified newspaper's story:

> *When in command of the war department grounds, it was my custom to escort the president nearly every night. He would come over to the war department early in the evening and I would return with him to the White House at any hour between 10 o'clock and 4 in the morning. Secretary Stanton would have me buckle on my sword belt and revolver and would send me off with the president. Lincoln wanted no guards, but the war secretary insisted that he was in personal danger if he did not have some protection.*

Mr. Jackson also talked about the president's "very mischievous son" Tad and of often finding that the boy had fallen asleep in Mr. Lincoln's office while awaiting the statesman's late-night return.

While in Washington, Lieutenant Jackson married Emma Lakin and took her home to North Haven. It was during that leave of absence that Mr. Lincoln was felled by a bullet to the head. "I took the first train for Washington and upon my arrival Mr. Stanton assigned me to the charge of forming the escort of officers who were to march in the procession," Jackson said in the newspaper story. Mr. Jackson resigned on May 22, 1865, as a twenty-one-year-old major.

His descendants are unsure about when Mr. Jackson became a New Yorker. His wife was only twenty-six when she died, and that was in 1872 in Connecticut. The 1894 letter quoted in *The Badge of Gallantry* was written on stationery of the Dewey House, Thousand Islands, and was mailed in Clayton, but he wrote a return address in New Haven.

Emma Jackson bore two daughters. One lived in Washington, and the other, Maude, was married in New Haven to a Yale student, Grant Erastus Crumb of Clayton, in 1885. Mr. Crumb returned to Clayton with his bride, eventually moving to Chaumont and, finally, to Smithville. Major Jackson was with them in Smithville for his last years of life. He is buried at Smithville Cemetery in a modestly marked grave. Grant E. Crumb died in 1927, and Maude died in December 1953.

When Cary R. Brick, then the chief of staff for Representative John M. McHugh (R–Pierrepont Manor), more recently secretary of the army under President Barack Obama, went to the National Archives to assist me in this war story, he came up with another interesting note about the old soldier. Major Jackson had to convince Washington that he had been awarded the Medal of Honor.

In a November 5, 1892 letter, Mr. Jackson wrote from New Haven, "It is with the greatest surprise that I have just learned…that my name did not appear" on a list of medal winners. In the letter, he described how Mr. Lincoln had directed Mr. Stanton to issue him the award.

The War Department responded within days, disclosing that "no record has been found that a Medal of Honor was granted you." He was asked to send the medal to Washington as evidence of his claim while officials researched his military records. He complied with the request. It seems astounding that Washington acted so quickly. In a letter dated November 28, 1892, Mr. Jackson was informed that his "name has been properly noted on the records of this Department in accordance with the facts stated in the inscription on the Medal of Honor," and the medal was returned to him.

The whereabouts of his medal are unknown to his descendants in Jefferson County. It may be with family in California. Or is it where it belongs, with his remains?

Material for this story was provided by Hilda Hayes of Smithville and Joyce Crumb of Adams, widows of the major's great-grandsons, Wenzell Hayes and Grant Edwin Crumb. The major's great-granddaughter, Virginia Crumb, and great-great-grandchildren—Emily Hayes, Joyce Hayes and Wenzell Hayes Jr.—also assisted. The unidentified newspaper, saved by Emily Hayes, may have been the National Tribune, *official newspaper of the Grand Army of the Republic, according to Mr. Heiser in Gettysburg.*

Barney Family Witnessed History and Made It

"Onward 24th," commanded Major Andrew Jackson Barney as he prodded his mount to the crest of a railroad embankment during the Second Battle of Bull Run. It was August 30, 1862, and his unit, the Twenty-fourth New York Infantry, was buckling in the face of fierce opposition. The soldier from Belleville, New York, intent on stopping any notions of retreat, pressed his spurs to the horse, sending man and beast to the prominent position to lead a charge. Then the twenty-four-year-old soldier turned in his saddle and shouted the words to rally his men.

"The words had hardly passed his lips when he fell backward, pierced by two balls," his eulogist, LaFayette J. Bigelow, said twenty-five days later at the officer's funeral on the fairgrounds in Belleville.

The story of local hero "Jack" Barney did not stop there. Hours after the battle, according to one source, he was recognized and rescued by one of the Confederacy's top military strategists, General Thomas J. "Stonewall" Jackson. Years earlier, one history writer suggested, Jack Barney had sat at the feet of this same soldier Jackson, possibly in a house in Henderson, New York, listening to old war stories. That Georgian-style house still stands on Route 178 in Henderson.

The Barney family of southern Jefferson County was entwined with well-known historical figures. For instance, one of Abraham Lincoln's confidants—allegedly an adviser for his Emancipation Proclamation—was Hiram Barney from southern Jefferson County.

Edgar Allan Poe's devotion to a Barney woman of Henderson was poetic. Marie Louise Barney Shew befriended the poet and assisted his dying bride.

General Jackson was a guest and patient of Dr. Lowrey Barney—Hiram's brother, Marie's father and Jack's cousin—staying in the house on Route 178. For that reason, as lore of the day asserted, the general recognized the fallen soldier at Bull Run.

Lowrey Barney was just a toddler, a one-year-old, when his parents, Daniel and Sarah—or Abigail, depending on which history we believe—moved in 1794 from Coventry, Rhode Island, to New York, initially settling in Herkimer. They moved north to Rutland and then shifted to Adams before finally, in 1807, making Henderson their home. Mrs. Barney gave birth to Hiram four years later.

Daniel, a physician, guided himself to the homes of his patients in what was the forestland of Henderson by following markings on trees, according to a series written in 1929 by *Watertown Daily Times* reporter Margaret Blakely. Like his dad, Lowrey chose to become a doctor and at sixteen became his father's understudy. He graduated in 1820 from the College of Physicians and Surgeons of Western New York and, in 1823, from Fairfield Medical College, Castleton, Vermont.

Hiram, on the other hand, chose a law career, which would help acquaint him with Lincoln before the "great emancipator" became president. He established his practice in New York City.

Lowrey Barney married Almira Spencer in 1821. He built for her and his growing family in 1827–28 the home that remains a landmark in Henderson. Almira left three children when she died about three weeks shy of her fortieth birthday in 1838. Pamelia Farrell Wallace, a thirty-five-year-old widow, became the doctor's second wife in 1843.

Almira had lived to see her firstborn child's wedding. Mary Louise was only sixteen when she married a physician, Joel Shew, in 1837. The couple moved to New York City, where Dr. Shew conducted a successful practice.

Dr. and Mrs. Shew were living at 47 Bond Street in New York when in 1846 Mrs. Shew was introduced to Edgar Allan Poe and his teenage bride, Virginia Clemm Poe, who were living in Fordham in the Bronx. Virginia was dying of tuberculosis, and Mrs. Shew made frequent visits to the Poe home carrying hampers of food and wine.

On the day before his wife's death, January 30, 1847, Poe wrote to Mrs. Shew, saying, "Her bosom is full to overflowing, like my own with a boundless inexpressible gratitude to you. Lest she may never see you more, she bids me say that she sends you her sweetest kiss of love and will die blessing you."

Mr. Poe was also suffering from the disease, and Mrs. Shew attended to him as well. In gratitude, he wrote "To M.L.S.," a poem that appeared in the *Home Journal*. Prose dedicated "To Marie Louise" appeared in *Columbian Magazine*. He also became a frequent visitor to her New York City home and was said to have been there when he wrote a draft of "The Bells." Poe biographer John Ingram interviewed Mrs. Shew and found in her diary notations indicating that she believed that she suggested some of the phrases for the poem.

Mrs. Shew eventually became alarmed with Poe's eccentricities and attempted to distance herself from him. She told Ingram that she sent a letter to Poe, telling him "in all candor that nothing would or could save him from a sudden death but a prudent life of calm, with a woman fond enough and strong enough to manage his work." The poet died on January 1, 1849, in Baltimore, Maryland.

Lowrey Barney was in New York in 1851, visiting the home of his widowed and remarried daughter, Marie Louise Shew Houghton, when his brother, Hiram, introduced him to a twenty-seven-year-old army officer. Hiram Barney was a good friend of then major Thomas J. Jackson and believed that his big brother might be able to assist Jackson, who was complaining of lingering indigestion problems (dyspepsia).

Major Jackson was intrigued by a treatment plan offered by Dr. Barney and asked to be taken on as a patient. But since the soldier's time was limited because of his next military assignment, he prevailed on the doctor to take him to Henderson immediately for treatment.

The two men boarded a steamboat on a July morning and headed up the Hudson River to Albany, New York, and then took a train to Sackets Harbor, New York. The doctor's carriage completed their trek to Henderson. "My father at once started Jackson on a careful diet, prepared by mother, and much stress was laid on the use of fresh buttermilk and freshly made corn bread," the physician's second daughter, Elva Barney, wrote in a letter to Jackson biographer Roy Bird Cook. "He spent six weeks in our home, was accustomed to take daily walks to Henderson Harbor, about a mile from our home."

In a 1911 account of the Jackson visit, the *Syracuse Herald* reported that "it is said by old residents of Henderson that he was given to wandering about the fields and was often seen standing upon some hillside for hours in apparently deep reflection."

Jackson made several friends during his brief stay "in spite of his quiet nature," Miss Barney said. "On his walks he often carried an umbrella, and curiously, kept a cup at the shore so that he could drink of the waters of Lake Ontario."

The doctor's orders also called for eating plenty of fruit and…getting married. Jackson continued following the Barney remedy after leaving Henderson—even to the extent of taking a bride two summers later—and sent another similarly afflicted soldier to Henderson for the treatment.

Elva recalled that the tall, slender and "very courtly" Jackson frequently talked of his experiences in the Mexican-American War, commanding the attention of her father and brothers. Although Elva did not say so, her cousin, Jack, then thirteen, may also have been a captive listener, Harry F. Landon implied in his 1932 *History of the North Country*.

Jack Barney was "the idol of the school" at Belleville's Union Academy, said his eulogist. He became a lawyer but abandoned his practice to return to the family farm. "The sedentary habits of a lawyer affected his health unfavorably," Mr. Bigelow said at the funeral. "But the principal reason of his decision was that he became disgusted with the drudgery, the routine, the perplexities of office business, and other distasteful features of a calling that thrives on the misfortunes of others."

Despite his membership in the region's minority Democratic Party, his popularity won him election in 1857 as Town of Ellisburg supervisor. He also became director of the Agricultural Insurance Company. With the outbreak of the Civil War, Jack bade farewell to his wife, two children and mother, recruited a regiment of Ellisburg men and, as their captain, led them away to become Company K of the Twenty-fourth Infantry. Early in 1862, he was promoted to major.

The eulogy described the soldier's fateful day:

> *His regiment was ordered to charge through a piece of woods. They did so, led by him. Coming upon an old railroad embankment, behind which the enemy were collected in great force, the men were greeted with a most destructive fire of musketry. The regiment faltered.*
>
> *At this moment, Major Barney, fearing his men would retreat, put spurs to his horse. The spirited animal leaped an intervening fence. Rider and*

> *horse stood on top of that embankment, in full view of, and only a few feet from the rebels. He turned in his saddle and shouted, "Onward, 24th."*

Seeing their leader struck down, his men were nevertheless inspired by his example, Bigelow said. "His men rushed on, but it was into the very jaws of death, and his little command vanished away, as it were, in the face of such fearful odds."

Jack Barney was a first cousin, once removed, of Lowrey and Hiram Barney. His father, Eliakim, was a son of Edward Barney, whose brother was Daniel, father of Lowrey and Hiram. His mother was Sarah Barney, who was a first cousin of Eliakim's from Vermont. Jack Barney left a nineteen-year-old daughter, Elizabeth, and a thirteen-year-old son, Edward. His widow, who later became Caroline Moody, died in October 1871.

Jack's eulogist, LaFayette Bigelow, was a district attorney of Jefferson County, a legislator, a deputy assessor of revenues and a junior partner in the ownership of the *Watertown Daily Times*, accomplishing all of this in a short adult life. He was only thirty-three when he died suddenly on January 13, 1870.

Three of Lowrey Barney's sons marched off to war, each carrying a letter written by their father to the attention of General Jackson should they fall into enemy hands. Perhaps Jack Barney tucked away a similar correspondence.

After the smoke had cleared from the battlefield and the wounded were being collected, his men who had survived the conflict found Major Barney to still be breathing. The mortally wounded warrior handed over his Bible and papers to one of the men and was heard to utter the last words, "Tell my wife I died doing my duty—that I commend my little ones to the care of God."

As the party attempted to return to Union lines with their dead and wounded, they fell into Confederate hands. And here, the story went, General Jackson viewed a body and recognized it to be that of a man he had met in the Henderson area.

According to the *Barney Family News*, a circular dated June 1989, Stonewall Jackson ordered that the body be embalmed and that the fallen hero's sword and belongings be preserved for his family. He then ensured that a man from Belleville safely passed through Confederate lines under a flag of truce to claim the body and bring it home.

One of Lowrey's sons, Daniel, also came home in a box. He died of disease in 1864 in a military hospital at the age of thirty-four. Brothers George and Fromundas lived to talk about their respective artillery and cavalry services.

When Dr. Lowrey Barney went to visit his brother's home in the Spuyten Duyvil section of the Bronx, he may have been provided the comfort of the same guest room used by a presidential hopeful named Lincoln, a secretary of state named James G. Blaine and a U.S. senator named Cushman Davis, himself a Henderson native. These three were among dignitaries who were visitors to the Hiram Barney home, Margaret Blakely wrote.

Hiram, a partner in the New York City law firm of Barney, Butler & Parsons, was a Republican with a background of supporting Free-Soil and abolitionist candidates when, in the summer of 1859, he went to Chicago on a business trip, according to a Thacher Proffitt & Wood LLP website. As a representative of mortgage trustees of the Chicago and Northern Railroad, he met another railroad lawyer, Lincoln.

Discovering common ground in their political philosophies, the two men developed a friendship that served both well on a professional level. Barney represented Lincoln's legal matters in New York, and Lincoln returned the favor in Illinois.

Early in 1860, with Lincoln now being touted as a presidential candidate, Barney hosted him in New York to introduce him to the powerful and influential of the East. The candidate stayed in the Barney home and was escorted by Barney, according to the website. The eventual election of Lincoln won Barney a political appointment as collector of customs of the port of New York. Barney was also among Lincoln advisers who gathered in Springfield, Illinois, to recommend potential appointees to the new president's cabinet. Margaret Blakely wrote that Hiram Barney was so close to the president that he "was called upon to assist in drafting the Emancipation Proclamation." But in his memoirs, Barney minimized his input.

"Now I think we will not be interrupted," Lincoln was quoted by Barney, according to the Thacher website. "I have something to show you which I think will please you." Barney continued, "He then drew from the left breast pocket of the dress coat which he wore a manuscript and read it to me. It was his first emancipation proclamation. He said he would be very thankful for any suggestion which he said he approved and would adopt."

The historic document was issued September 22, 1862. There is no mention of Hiram Barney's apparent involvement in the Emancipation Proclamation in the 1995 book *Lincoln* by David Herbert Donald. The author discussed, however, the agony that the president endured when he was compelled to remove Barney from the New York port post: "Lincoln liked Barney and had confidence in his honor and integrity, but suspecting that the collector had 'eased to be master of his position,' proposed sending him as minister to Portugal." In 1864, President Lincoln yielded to political pressure because of problems occurring in the port administration and "with some reluctance, ousted Hiram Barney," Donald wrote.

A brief notice in a Jefferson County newspaper about Mr. Barney's death on May 18, 1895, in the Bronx noted that he resigned from the port position, "declining an appointment to a foreign mission."

When Dr. Lowrey Barney died on December 17, 1884, his daughter, Elva, inherited his house. She deeded the dwelling in 1907 to a niece, Mary Sawyer Houghton, daughter of Marie Louise Shew Houghton, but continued to live there until her death on February 18, 1937. She was eighty-seven.

Following the 1942 death of Mary Houghton Overton, the property was sold to E. June Scott. Five years later, Edward and Joyce Stuckey purchased the site. Victor and Bessie Scott became the property owners in 1950, and in the subsequent sixty-plus years, their son and daughter-in-law, Merrill and Nina Scott, presided over the old Barney estate.

Margaret G. Blakely, a Yonkers native and 1927 graduate of Syracuse University, was with the Watertown Daily Times *from 1928 to 1930, and during that tenure, she interviewed Eleanor Roosevelt in Carthage. Blakely was later an editorial assistant with MacMillan Company in New York. She died at eighty-six on March 30, 1989.*

Assisting in collection of material for this story were Mary Demianenko of the Historical Association of South Jefferson, Eric C. Anderson of the Henderson Historical Society and Elizabeth Barney Millard of Woodville, who provided Genealogy of the Barney Family in America, *published by Eugene Dimon Preston and William Clifford Barney. Information was also obtained from Harold I. Sanderson's Civil War website and from the files of Jefferson County Surrogate Court.*

Flash and Fortitude

The Military Magruders

There was a story told decades ago in military circles about an officer's grand feast at a Northern New York outpost, put on to impress his uniformed British guests from across the Canadian border. He had already seen a lavish display of silver and etiquette when he was toasted on the Canadian side. Surely this man, dubbed "Prince John" because of his theatrical flamboyance, wanted to measure up when he returned the favor. The fact that Prince John "owed money to everybody in the Army" wasn't about to stop him, wrote Gordon G. Heiner Jr., a Madison Barracks officer, in 1938.

From other officers, it was said, he borrowed gold and silver plates, cut glassware and ornate furniture. What he couldn't borrow, Prince John rented. The invitations he sent his counterparts across the border were engraved, and he had stylish carriages to taxi the visitors about. Queen Victoria's officers were impressed indeed as they dined.

The legend continues that one of the Englishmen leaned over to his host and asked, "Say old chap, what may I ask is your monthly pay?"

"Damned if I know," the mustachioed American answered. "We turn over our pay to our thervants," he lisped.

Mr. Heiner, the first historian for Madison Barracks, reported that the grand affair took place in the stone house that once served as the Sackets Harbor quarters for Ulysses S. Grant.

I'm here to set the record straight. Our apologies to the late Mr. Heiner, but from the evidence I have, Prince John neither feasted at Madison

"Prince John" Magruder, once stationed at Madison Barracks in Sackets Harbor, New York, later became a general in the Confederate army. *Courtesy* Watertown Daily Times.

Lawson W. Magruder III, former commanding general at Fort Drum, New York, can say that the Confederate general was his third cousin, three times removed. *Courtesy* Watertown Daily Times.

Barracks nor ever breathed the air blowing off Lake Ontario to the shores of western Jefferson County.

Prince John was John Bankhead Magruder, a United States soldier who fought against the Seminole Indians and in the Mexican-American War, and later he was a Confederate general. If the name Magruder rings a bell, it is with good reason. An eventual commanding general at Fort Drum, New York, Lawson W. Magruder III is related to the courtly officer who once actually ranked at Plattsburgh.

John Bankhead Magruder was the third cousin, three times removed, of the latter-day soldier. According to a genealogy compiled and updated by the Magruder generations, John's great-great-grandfather, William Magruder, was a brother of Lawson Magruder's great-great-great-great-great-grandfather.

Prince John Magruder "loved to play host," wrote a biographer, Mark Grimsley.

> *Elegance was etched in every line in his face, every move of his body. His erect stance, florid complexion, and jet-black mustache belied his 51 years* [in 1861]. *His eyes flashed with dramatic, almost Latin fire. He was unabashedly exotic and had an aristocrat's disdain for humdrum convention. He made a festival of life, and although he had many betters as a military man, for sheer gusto no one could beat John Bankhead Magruder.*
>
> *Magruder's speech matched his appearance: courtly, impressive, sparkling. Only a slight lisp marred his otherwise perfect elocution.*

It is easy enough to believe that John Magruder ruled at Sackets, since Mr. Heiner said so, though vaguely, in his 1938 Madison Barracks history, *From Saints to Red Legs*. He provided no time period and offered no other reference to the officer. He wrote, "The old stone house, part of which Grant is said to have occupied, was the one in which Prince John Magruder, who was stationed here sometime before the Civil War, gave his magnificent entertainments."

To the contrary, Paul D. Casdorph, author of *Prince John Magruder, His Life & Campaigns*, published in 1996, places the prince and his feast at Plattsburgh. It was a new post to which First Lieutenant Magruder was assigned in the fall of 1838, and it was a hotel room that served as his quarters. He bid farewell to New York winters in March 1840, when his First Artillery moved to Maine.

Later, during the Mexican-American War (1846–48), he impressed his superiors while commanding a light artillery battery, and within that two-year span, he had won successive promotions to major and lieutenant colonel. But he also showed his recklessness while on the Mexican front. He got into a dispute with a brigadier general over a card game, according to the Grimsley narrative, and challenged the general to a duel. The face-off never materialized, enabling Americans to eventually elect the general, Franklin Pierce, president of the United States.

One last note about John Bankhead Magruder: his achievements as a leader in battle were mixed, but his talent for deception paid off once for the Confederacy. Three days after the April 17, 1861 secession of his state, Virginia, from the Union, he resigned his commission in the army and put on the gray uniform of the South. As brigadier general eleven months later, he was left to defend Yorktown and Richmond with an army dwarfed by the forces of Union general George McClellan.

McClellan has gone down in history as the indecisive general who failed to attack. Perhaps less heralded is Magruder's trickery in disguising his actual strength. "From the moment the first Yankee scouts appeared before his lines, he [Magruder] exercised his special talents and stage-managed his 11,000 men into a force seemingly far more formidable," wrote McClellan biographer Stephen W. Sears in 1988. "The illusion Magruder created no doubt had its effect."

General Lawson Magruder, who held the Fort Drum command from 1997 to 1999 and retired from the army in 2001, expressed cautious pride in the Confederate service of not only his distant cousin but also his great-grandfather, Major Lawson W. Magruder, and another distant cousin, Thomas S. Magruder, who was a war casualty. "Yes, there's pride," he said. "I don't believe in their cause, but I'm proud that they had the conviction to serve and bear arms for what they believed…And I'm glad that they lost." Adding to that pride is the knowledge that once the Civil War ended, his ancestors became good productive Americans, he said. The major had five sons who wore United States military uniforms. One was a navy rear admiral who gave his life in World War I.

Military service in the Magruder family is a tradition. In fact, the keepers of the Magruder genealogy have linked their kinship all the way back to Alpin MacAchaia, crowned king of the Scots in AD 833. This king, killed in battle at Avrshire, left three sons, including Gregor MacAlpin, who is "pretty generally claimed" to be founder of the "Clan Gregor."

The evolving generations, with name spinoffs of McGruder and McCruder, appeared in the seventeenth and eighteenth centuries. When Charles II invaded England in 1651, three of his warriors were James, Alexander and John McGruder. The brothers were taken prisoners, and the following year, they were sent to the American colonies as indentured servants.

Alexander was General Magruder's great-great-great-great-great-great-great-grandfather. Alexander's fourth-generation descendant, Ninian Beall Magruder, fought in the Revolutionary War. In fact, his name is among thirty-one Magruders, all of Alexander's line, who are memorialized in Montgomery County, Maryland, for fighting in the war for independence. At the risk of beating the drum too long, I am obliged to report that General Magruder's father, a resident of Waco, Texas, saw combat in World War II, Korea and Vietnam.

Despite the military background, the army officer said that there was no pressure on him to carry on the tradition. "The defining experience for me was in 1958, when I was eleven. Dad was in Paris, and he took my sister and me to Normandy, where he landed on Utah Beach on D-Day. We retraced his steps, and I saw a real emotional side of my father as he vividly recalled places up to August 2, 1944, when he was seriously wounded…I told myself then that I wanted to be a part of my father's chosen profession."

General Magruder viewed the movie *Saving Private Ryan* and said that it renewed the emotions he saw forty years ago. "It reminded me that my father's generation saved the world as we know it today. Where would we be today without the sacrifices that they made?…As I watch his generation pass on, I feel the American public should reach out one more time to express appreciation to an incredible generation that served in uniform."

Reference was made earlier to Gordon G. Heiner Jr. His booklet *From Saints to Red Legs* went on sale in 1938, a culmination of not only his three years of research for the first history written about Madison Barracks but also his four-year tenure at the Sackets Harbor outpost. He was a major at Madison Barracks, in charge of planning and training of the Fifth Field Artillery. A veteran of both world wars, he retired as a colonel in 1948 and died in 1961 at Walter Reed Army Medical Center.

The site where Prince John's feast was *not* served, the former quarters of U.S. Grant, still stands. Dinner was actually served there decades later in a restaurant called Old Stone Row.

About the Author

As Dave Shampine completes his forty-first year as crime reporter and history writer with the *Watertown Daily Times* in Northern New York, he provides his fourth offering to The History Press in this collection of Civil War stories. He made his debut with The History Press in 2009 with *Remembering New York's North Country: Tales from Times Gone By* and then followed in 2010 with two publications: *Colorful Characters of Northern New York: Northern Lights* and the work to which he was dedicated for more than a decade, *The North Country Murder of Irene Izak: Stained by Her Blood.*

A native of Carthage, New York, and a lifetime resident of Jefferson County, New York, Mr. Shampine takes pride in his education at Carthage Augustinian Academy, Jefferson Community College—where in 2007 he was honored with a professional achievement award—Franklin Pierce College in New Hampshire and the State University of New York College at Brockport.

He has also been a contributor to the Jefferson County Historical Society's *Bulletin* and to *Inland Seas*, the quarterly journal of the Great Lakes Historical Society, Vermillion, Ohio.